Saving France in the 1580s

PETER LANG
New York • Washington, D.C./Baltimore • Bern
Frankfurt • Berlin • Brussels • Vienna • Oxford

JAMES H. DAHLINGER

Saving France in the 1580s

WRITINGS OF ETIENNE PASQUIER

PETER LANG
New York • Washington, D.C./Baltimore • Bern
Frankfurt • Berlin • Brussels • Vienna • Oxford

Library of Congress Cataloging-in-Publication Data

Dahlinger, James H.
Saving France in the 1580s: writings of Etienne Pasquier / James H. Dahlinger.
pages cm
Includes bibliographical references and index.
1. Pasquier, Etienne, 1529–1615—Political and social views.
2. Pasquier, Etienne, 1529–1615—Influence. 3. Historians—France—Biography. 4. Poets, French—16th century—Biography. 5. Lawyers—France—Biography. 6. France—History—16th century—Historiography.
7. Nationalism—France—History—16th century. 8. France—Politics and government—1562–1598. 9. Law—Social aspects—France—History—16th century. I. Title.
DC112.P3D36 944'.029092—dc23 2012039904
ISBN 978-1-4331-2063-3 (hardcover)
ISBN 978-1-4539-0963-8 (e-book)

Bibliographic information published by **Die Deutsche Nationalbibliothek**.
Die Deutsche Nationalbibliothek lists this publication in the "Deutsche Nationalbibliografie"; detailed bibliographic data is available on the Internet at http://dnb.d-nb.de/.

Portrait of Pasquier on the cover is from
Dorothy Thickett, *Bibliography of Works of Estienne Pasquier* (1956) © Librairie Droz

29 Broadway, 18th floor, New York, NY 10006
www.peterlang.com

CONTENTS

Acknowledgments	vii
1. Introduction	1
2. Pasquier's Self-Fashioning as the Ideal Public Servant	13
3. Law, Custom and the Individual, Revisited in the *Pourparlers*	33
4. Law and the Christian Tradition in France	65
5. Pasquier's Reception in Posterity	87
6. Conclusions	103
Notes	109
Bibliography	119
Index	123

ACKNOWLEDGMENTS

I would like to thank editors Marie-Madeleine Fragonard and François Roudaut for their monumental edition of Etienne Pasquier's *Recherches de la France*, from Editions Champion, which partially inspired this project about Pasquier's contributions to peace and continuity of law in his time. I thank Editions Champion for permission to reprint from the Fragonard and Roudaut volumes. I thank Professor Nancy Regalado of New York University for much good advice. I'd like to thank Editions Droz for their permanently useful editions of Pasquier's correspondence, as well as for permission to reprint from those volumes; the always helpful staffs of the Bibliothèque Nationale in Paris and New York University and Columbia University libraries; the encouragement of colleagues and members of the annual Sixteenth Century Studies Conference; Professor Moya Arthur and Professor Robert Cousineau SJ for showing interest in my work. I also wish to thank Le Moyne College, Syracuse for providing me a sabbatical year to work on this project, and also the Jesuit Community of Loyola Hall, Fordham University for kind support during that sabbatical, as well as for access to the Fordham University libraries. Many thanks to the excellent staff of Peter Lang Publishing Inc., especially my wonderful production editor Jackie Pavlovic. Finally I reserve my warmest thanks for my sister, Susan E. Dahlinger, an author and editor in nineteenth century studies, for much advice and support.

· 1 ·
INTRODUCTION

Assemblée des Trois Estats Tenue en la Ville de Blois, 1588

Pendant qu'icy d'une magnifique arroy
Chacun de vous à l'envy sacrifie
(Docte prelat) et sa mort et sa vie
Pour restablir nostre ancienne loy.
Moy cependant qui ne suis point à moy
Poulse du vent d'une longue follie,
Je me repars d'une philosophie
Qui tient mon ame, et mes sens en esmoy
Bien que d'amour je suive le guidon,
Jamais, (Thiart) je ne tiray guerdon
De celle-là qui est ma mieux aimée.
Face le ciel que tout ce beau traffic
Que remuez pour le repos public,
Comme mon feu, ne se tourne en fumee.[1]

Pasquier dedicates this verse to *Thiart*,[2] who was a friend and the senior poet of the *Pléïade*, as well as bishop of Châlon. The two poets share a mood of apprehension about the future, a mood then pervasive among thinkers. As he and fellow parliamentarians attend the Estates of Blois in 1588, he is anxious to *restablir nostre ancienne loy*. Pasquier, when questioned by fellow parliamentarians as to what degree one ought to risk oneself in loyalty to the king and to the established order, had replied on the vein of this verse: *chacun de vous à l'envy sacrifie et sa mort et sa vie*. He believed that the State and the rightful order of things were worthy of one's own ultimate self-sacrifice. We know that he did follow Henri III into exile at Tours to establish a government in exile when Paris was under siege by the *Ligue*. The duty of the citizen is clear: "moy qui ne suis point à moy" indicates the quality of disinterested loyalty he prescribes for the good citizen—"le bon français." French law, which for him and the Parisan *bareau* is a cement of good morals and public order, has been compromised by a complexity of forces: Italian dominance in government posts; venality; the Spanish menace; post-Tridentine assertions by the papacy on the affairs of the Gallican Church; the Wars of Religion with the aggravations of the *Ligue*. The disorder has swept the nation headlong in its chaotic path: *Poulse du vent d'une longue follie*. Pasquier writes to remind his fellow citizens, and also future generations, *posterité*, about the central importance of law and cultural tradition to maintain the self-concept of the French, the well-being of citizens and of the secure continuity of the State. Pasquier's readership then is exhorted to engage in self-renewal in loyalty to traditionally French values.

Etienne Pasquier was a renowned lawyer and magistrate who carefully worked to construct his *persona* as a moral and cultural center of the parliament of Paris, and thus he sought to place his stamp on French law and public life. Chapter 2 of this book describes Pasquier's strategies of self-fashioning. After some debate over the year of his birth (some indications gave the year 1528), it can be concluded that he was in all probability born June 7, 1529 in Paris, and died there in 1615. Paul Bouteiller offers full details about the Pasquiers' genealogy[3]: The first known member of the family was Jean Pasquier, who had commanded a regiment of infantry at the siege of Pampluna. In 1460 the Pasquiers had constructed for themselves the mortuary chapels of St. Cyprien and Ste. Barbe in the church of Saint-Séverin, in the Paris locality on the left bank, where Etienne spent his early years. This is also one of the first extant mentions of the Pasquier name. Etienne was the only issue of the marriage of Antoine Pasquier and Philippe Clément. Antoine had followed his father Jean in a military career and was styled a *bourgeois de Paris*. It can be reasonably supposed that Antoine had met his wife, Philippe Clément, since both families had country estates in proximity to one another.[4]

Little else is known of the parents, though Antoine Pasquier must have enjoyed sufficient political and social connections to provide for his son Etienne the very type of the ideal educational itinerary of his time, which was necessary to build a successful future career in law and in the high magistracy. Etienne Pasquier was sent by his father to the College de Presle where he attended courses of his uncle, Adrien Tournèbe and possibly Peter Ramus. It was at Presle that he met Antoine Loisel and Pierre Pithou, both of whom would become permanent, like-minded friends and associates in the Parliament. We know that the law led to all forms of advancement in Pasquier's time. This point is perhaps best echoed in a citation from Loisel's own father advising him in that vocation as opposed to medicine: "As a physician one is always *just* a physican but in the law one can also become a president or a chancellor." It is a matter of dispute to what degree Pasquier actually knew Ramus, at Presle, as he claims in his published *Correspondence*. Catherine Magnien has recently made a study suggesting that Pasquier may well have invented his close association with him.[5] Antoine Loisel *was* on close terms with Ramus and became executor of his estate after his death during the Sainte-Barthelémy.

The renowned Law Faculty of Toulouse, under *Le grand* Cujas, was another mandatory part of the distinguished trajectory of Pasquier's studies that he also experienced with friends Pithou and Loisel. They also attended lectures of Bauduin and Hotman. He made the requisite tour of Italy, studying in Bologna under Socinus, and in Pavia, under Alciatus. Pasquier wrote to Pithou that in his last years as a young student as well as during his first introduction to the Paris bar, and before he began to plead cases, he "made books" that were in keeping with his youth: The pastoral love casuistry narrative *le Monophile* appeared in 1554, and the *lettres amoureuses* and the *Colloques d'Amour*, both in 1555. By 1560 appeared the first two books of his major work, *Les Recherches de la France*[6] together with a dialogue, the *Pourparler du prince*. I examine the *Pourparler du prince* and two other similar works, *The Pourparler de la loy* and the *Pourparler d'Alexandre* in chapter 3; while chapter 4 discusses contents of Book III of the *Recherches de la France*, where Pasquier uses vignettes of French Church history which he relates to the events of the contemporary Civil Wars of Religion to teach ecclesiastical and religious ethics. Pasquier had very personal reasons to be concerned with keeping the peace in regard to religion, as some colleagues and his own wife had been victims of the extremist right-wing Catholic *Ligue*.

In 1557 he married a wealthy young widow, Françoise Belen for whom he had won a substantial lawsuit. The couple had five sons and one daughter together: Theodore, Nicolas, Pierre, Guy and René and Françoise, who perhaps for the usual discretion around speaking about female relatives, he never mentions more than by name. She may have died quite young or entered a convent.

As Pasquier began his apprenticeship at the Paris bar, he ate some poisonous mushrooms at his country estate which necessitated a long recuperation. While convalescing in the country, he met two members of the University of Paris, MMs Beguin and Levasseur, who he was to include in the introductory matter of his *Pourparler du prince*. These same interlocutors were to be responsible for the University's selection of Pasquier as defense counsel in its case against the Jesuits in 1564. In chapter 2 on Pasquier's self-fashioning, I suggest that he admits that his acceptance of the case was the first step towards his success: "*la premiere planche de mon advancement au Palais*." While it is always asserted by Pasquier himself and by historians that he vehemently disapproved of the Jesuits, when in fact most of the French establishment welcomed their efforts in establishing their schools throughout the realm, it was undeniably in Pasquier's interests—*encouraged* as he was by his Gallican, parliamentarian senior colleagues—that he defend the University against the Jesuit cause. Had he declined to do so, on whatever account, his "advancement" in the ranks of the *robins* might well have been more circuitous. Although the University ultimately lost its case because of the king's intervention, Pasquier would decide to profit by an ambient anti-Jesuitism that lingered in *robin* circles, for the balance of his career, while privately communicating on congenial terms with individual Jesuits. Pasquier always focused on establishing himself with pride of place in the Paris *Parlement*.

Pasquier was well established at the Paris *Parlement* when he was also chosen to preside the *Grands Jours* in Poitiers in 1567 and again in 1579 as well as those of Troyes in 1583. He and his colleagues worked on a back-log of civil and criminal cases in what was actually a *survivance* of the ancient peripatetic Parliament.[7] It was during his residence in Poitiers that he would participate in the salon of Madeleine and Catherine Des Roches, mother and daughter. The community of poets that the salon constituted produced collective works, "La Puce de Madame Des Roches," and "La Main," focused on the synecdoche of Pasquier's hands, these latter not shown, in the celebrated De Hoey portrait of him. In both of these collective works, Pasquier plays a central role and also served as their editor. By the time of the *Grands Jours*, Pasquier had developed a reputation as a poet. Pasquier's *Recherches de la France*, books VII and VIII in particular show him to have been well acquainted with what he termed *les anciennetez de la France*—in his admiration for medieval French verse. In this he was part of a contemporary trend, with other *robin* colleagues, especially Claude Fauchet.[8] His friends Loisel and Pithou also joined in research and publication of their own works in the trend of les *antiquitez*. But Pasquier also had high esteem for contemporary French poets, especially for friendships he had made among the poets of the *Pléïade*.

Indeed Pasquier was fond of a number of medieval poets and their poetics. He is as interested in the ethical and cultural value of these poets and their message, as he makes clear in Book VII of the *Recherches*, as in their cultivation of the discipline of their poetics. In this latter point his taste runs countercurrent to the ideals enunciated in Du Bellay's manifesto, the *Défense et illustration*. He states unambiguously at the same time, in Book VII of his *Recherches* that while France has always boasted of fine poets whose talents were on a par with those of Rome, he prefers the *modern* trends as may be seen among the "flotte de bons poetes depuis le regne de notre roi Henri II."[9] We have seen his admiration for Tyard, and he befriended Ronsard, the recognized leader of the *Pléïade*, and was his correspondent. In his own poetical exercises he espouses *Pléïade* ideals of imitation, wide-ranging reading in the poets, and a desire to enhance the capacities of the French vernacular to express the full range of esthetic and abstract concepts. In addition, he imitates Ronsard in both his verse forms and themes as well as in his work ethic, inherited by the *Pléïade* from their master, Jean Dorat,[10] that one should practice French, and perhaps also Latin verse on a daily basis. Pasquier writes that at the end of a busy day at the *bareau*, he would pen French or Latin epigrams. He also imitates the grand trajectory of Ronsard's own poetical career in that, like the poet *vendômois*, he began "making books" as he says, of love poetry, and gradually evolved, in his poetry of circumstances to embrace the cause of national solidarity and the integrity of French identity during the crisis of the Civil Wars of Religion. This increasingly urgent need to shore up national institutions in the face of the menaces we have discussed, became a driving impetus for virtually all of Pasquier's writing. He used his writing to teach ethics and the responsibility of king and citizen alike to encourage identity with pride with all things French and to preserve and defend the kingdom in its laws and in its traditional, identifiable culture. In keeping with the *Pléïade's* interest in neologisms and also influenced by Rabelais and Bovelles,[11] he devotes parts of Book I of his *Recherches*, in his discussion of his (then original) theory about the

Gaulish origins of France and of French institutions, to speculation about the Gaulish etymological origins of specific words. Largely inspired by Bovelles[12] and Estienne, he devotes Book VIII of his *Recherches* to an exploration of traditional French proverbs, words and phrases that had descended into the popular consciousness and to individual words and proper names. He discusses the word "Huguenot" in reference to the religious reformers whose numbers had not ceased to grow throughout the 1560s to the 80s. Pasquier, who will declare himself a moderate for the sake of restoring peace after the Civil Wars, also attaches this term, Huguenot to the conspiracy of Amboise, during the minority of François II. He uses this historical vignette as he does others, throughout his works, to illustrate an ethics of tolerance and moderation: modes to adopt or conduct to avoid in the interests of the continuity of the State. Of course, much had happened since the 1560 exhortations of Michel de l'Hospital in favor of peaceful and responsible citizenship.[13] *Discontinuity* had become something of a norm. Pasquier knew that he had to modify his own prejudices against the Reformers' movements, and encourage all others to do so, if *Parlement* was to maintain order and preserve the realm. His sense of continuity then had to take account of the *rupture* represented by the nine successive Wars of Religion, and that the ideal of *un roi, une loi, une foi* would need a new, more inclusive interpretation.[14] In chapter 3 of this book, I analyze Pasquier's own interpretation, no doubt guided by advice from parliamentarian peers, on how *la foy* (faith) has served the continuity and flourishing of what Pasquier refers to as France's *monarchie de marque*. He explains the traditional response to faith and Church as one which is still valid, and indeed urgently needed in his own day. Pasquier and his parliamentarian peers view the Church in France as one of the institutions of the monarchy, like the University, and the *Parlement* itself. The Church he describes is the *Catholique, apostolique et romaine*, and while he acknowledges his own allegiance to that church, and, in his manner acknowledges the *spiritual* primacy of the popes (a point to which we will return), he will make a *Gallican* case for the king's ultimate authority over all French church affairs. He articulates his views not with a theological or spiritual lexicon *per se* but rather with a legal and historical one, as befits his training. French religious *praxis* is strongly allied to customary law and is deeply rooted in national culture; it is then imperative to Pasquier that Frenchmen adhere to traditional, *Gallican* norms in relationship to Church, to Rome and give a very specific, negative response to the divisions contemporaries often found inherent in religious *nouveauté*. The divisions manifest in the Civil Wars are a large part then of Pasquier's impetus in writing Book III, in which he continues his methodology, familiar throughout the *Recherches de la France:* as he popularizes French ecclesiastical history, choosing to write in the vernacular, he gives vignettes from that history to disseminate *Gallican* ethics and attitudes. He is well read in French ecclesiastical history, ancient Roman and Canon law and French Customary law. He and his colleagues in the *Parlement*, Pithou, Loisel and others will have completed the writing down for the first time of Paris Customary law. We see from the outset of Book III a *survivance* of the medieval blending of theology, doctrinal apologetics and Regalian law, and that the Christian Scriptures are a normative aspect of that development.

Pasquier's contents in Book III could be termed a *catechisme des Gallicans*, a case for royal and parliamentary control of ecclesiastical affairs; just as he also developed his strident work of invective, the *Catéchisme des jésuites*. In both cases, he bends historical realities to suit his purpose, and while critics such as George Huppert[15] have praised him as a herald of modern history, relying more objectively on evidence; still we see in his treatment of ecclesiastical affairs that he is still not himself completely removed from the self-interest and ambition which he decries in a Paolo Giovio, a Froissart, or a Commynes, to cite some examples. Just as his opposition to the Jesuits is informed by his project of self-construction, or if one will, *self-fashioning* to promote his ascent in the *Parlement*, so we find the same goals at work in his writing in Book III about the rights and privileges of the Gallican Church. It was not without interest for Pasquier that his colleagues Pierre Pithou and Jacques-Auguste de Thou also produced treatises on Gallican rights.[16]

It is the premise of this book that as we examine Pasquier's self-construction as always woven into his motivations in what he writes, we see that he wants to persuade his reader that law and traditional culture are imperative to shore up the State in times of uncertainty. This then is his motive in writing Book III of his *Recherches*. At the time of the publication of this work he still wants to persuade that there ought to be one Church only, the traditional Roman Catholic Apostolic one, though the Church should be thoroughly informed and governed by Gallican principles. He appeals once again to historic precedent to argue his case. He will appeal to the foundational actions of Christ Himself as recorded in the Gospels.[17] He also traces for his reader a *précis* of developments in ecclesiology and in other points of doctrine in both the Apostolic and the Patristic ages.

In his discussion of the development of Church history and doctrine, he is grateful that Western Christianity never experienced the heresies that plagued the Eastern Churches. In this he seems to unite his discussion of the French national ecclesiastical experience to that of the parliamentary monarchy which he discussed in Book II of his *Recherches*. A well known phrase of Pasquier's, "Nous seuls," is his *leitmotif* throughout Book II and indeed in all his writings, i.e., that while other kingdoms and empires have risen and subsequently fallen, France's "monarchie de marque" is the only one to have endured over time. Similarly, the Western Church (and Pasquier's emphasis of course will be on the French Church as an arm of the monarchy) like Parliament he pursues in Book III, has developed without the Christological heresies that bring divisions. In this he draws a parallel with the divisions brought by the "diversité de' religions," in his own time. These he also characterizes as "sectes dangereux," the Lutheran, Calvinist and Jesuit phenomena. While in his correspondence he speaks of Geneva, "source de tous nos maux." He will find that the Jesuits, because of their prior, ultra-montaine allegiances of the time, were no less dangerous for national unity and security than the Protestant movements, and in this he enlists the Gallican argument that France and her kings have always enjoyed the rights and privileges ("droits et privileges") which historically had been negotiated and accepted by most popes.

Pasquier traces the development of the doctrine of papal primacy and of the preeminence of the See of Rome over those of Antioch, Constantinople and Jerusalem. He also declares that, ultimately, France had been instrumental in establishing and maintaining popes in their authority. For their aid to the Papacy, kings had gradually accrued rights and privileges to name bishops, to call Councils, to be free from the threat of interdict, and generally to control the internal affairs of the Church in France. Still Pasquier, speaking also for his parliamentary colleagues, claims to recognize the priority of papal authority in *spiritual*, not temporal matters. These latter are the province of the French king (informed by the *Parlement*). Pasquier's casuistry leads him to torture the logic of Christian doctrine, which states that human acts placed in the temporal sphere are informed in their goodness by the primacy of the *unseen*, the spiritual. That is, works are made possible by Grace, which also inspires faith. Temporal acts are to be informed by the individual's free response to the *Decalogue*, to the *Beatitudes* and to the Laws of the Church, all in cooperation with Grace. Pasquier, however, goes so far as to interpret the scriptural words of Christ to suit his own *Gallican* agenda. In the scriptural narrative, Christ declares to Pilate that His kingdom is not of this world. Therefore, Pasquier argues, Christ Himself did not claim authority over the business of this world, but only over the spiritual realm. Although Pasquier here sets up an untenable argument from the point of view of Christian doctrine, he is aware of the political ambitions of popes historically, who after all were themselves temporal princes. One point about Book III that is most salient is that Pasquier, who comes down to us as a figure of political and religious tolerance, here makes no allowance for a possible religious pluralism. We also see here, particularly in regard to the Jesuits that, as was frequent in the polemics of the day, he even deploys invective to discredit them. Thus as has been remarked already about the chancellor, Michel de l'Hospital, that he was not quite the tolerant figure as so often described, may also be said of Pasquier, at the time of the writing of Book III. He will exhort to tolerance in the late 1580s and beyond, as we see particularly recorded in his occasional verse; but it is also perhaps not insignificant that his ofttimes strident language in opposition to the new disparity of *religions* is not softened in subsequent editions of his *Recherches* or his *Correspondence*. The same strident language and tone will recur among his descendants, both familial and political.

Chapter 5 of this book discusses Pasquier's reception in posterity. It will be remembered that his efforts in publications and in his public life were always centered on both his self-fashioning and the advice he wanted to give about the ethics of *un bon français*, as well as the maintenance of a *monarchie de marque*, as he termed it, for the benefit not only of contemporaries but also of *posterité*. Enthusiasm for Pasquier's editions continued strong through the first half of the seventeenth century, while earlier, the work of invective opposing him posthumously, published by Jesuit Father François Garasse: *Les Recherches des Recherches et autres Oeuvres de M. Estienne Pasquier, pour la défense de nos Roys, contre les outrages, calomnies et autres impertinences dudit auteur*. Paris, by Sebastien Chappelet, 1622 had its effect in decreasing in a gradual sense, the popularity of Pasquier's works. In addition, Pasquier's son Nicolas' acerbic reply to Garasse: *Les Lettres de Nicolas Pasquier, fils d'Estienne . . . Avec la response aux Recherches des Recherches*, Paris, chez Gervais Alliot, 1623. Nicolas's response to Garasse which was reprinted in the Trévoux Collection of Pasquier's works in 1723,[18] perhaps hampered Nicolas's ascent as a successful author. This is a point that requires further critical attention. After relatively little authorial attention paid to Pasquier and his works in the eighteenth century, with the notable exception of Voltaire, the nineteenth century will see a resurgence of interest in him both as the moral compass of Parliamentarians and good citizens, and as a talented author of enduring appeal. In 1847, the Duke Etienne-Denis Pasquier, then chancellor of France and no doubt Etienne Pasquier's most distinguished descendant, published posthumously Etienne Pasquier's last lengthy work, the *Interpretation des Institutes de Justinien*. We will see that the chancellor had very definite motivations for this unique publication of the *Institutes* that point to the renewed prestige, in the period, both of Etienne Pasquier's memory, and of the *Parlement* of Paris. Pasquier was appreciated as an author also, once again.

Léon Feugère, a professor of Rhetoric at the *Lycée Descartes* who valued the works of French Renaissance authors, edited excerpts of Pasquier's *Recherches de la France* and of his *Correspondence* in his *Oeuvres Choisies*, in two volumes, in 1849. In the second volume of Feugère's work, *Maitre*, Claude Dupin contributes a lyrical, romantic *éloge* of Pasquier as a model of virtue in public life and of all things French. Sainte-Beuve also takes advantage of what we may speak of as the renewed Pasquier *mode*, by including him, with a critical appraisal, in his *Causeries du lundi*. The mid-to-late nineteenth century would be perhaps the last *élan* of Pasquier's appeal as a popular author or as a voice of ethical and political rectitude. In the twentieth and twenty-first centuries Pasquier, to paraphrase the literary critic Harold Bloom speaking of Virgil, has become an author of the professors and scholars, and so far, relatively few of those. A chief focus, most notably in the work of George Huppert, has been his innovations in historiography and his use of primary sources, as well as his practice of suspended judgment about the veracity of received views about origins of the French nation. While Dorothy Thickett is the great pioneer in modern Pasquier studies, and a number of individual works of Pasquier's have been the object of critical attention, it was not until the efforts of François Roudaut, Marie-Madeleine Fragonard, Catherine Magnien and company in 1996 that a fine, 3-volume critical edition appeared of *Les Recherches de la France*. Claude Sutto did fine service in his critical edition of Pasquier's *Catéchisme des jésuites*. Finally Béatrice Sayhi-Périgot produced her critical edition of the *Pourparlers*. I am grateful to all of these scholars and others and I make use of all of their editions in the current book, which is a companion to my *Etienne Pasquier on Ethics and History*. In that book I gave a detailed study of Pasquier's life in a more traditional biographical form, and I studied his use of the rhetorical devices of the *speculum principis* in the *Recherches*, as well as the self-portrait for emulation found woven into his correspondence with his friend and colleague Pierre Pithou. In Chapter six of this book I propose my conclusions. This book studies in a close reading, in English, Pasquier's self-fashioning in his strategic life choices and in some of his writings that have received less critical attention. It is hoped that the discussions here will encourage others to read Pasquier, who helps to give one entrance into the spectrum of events in late-sixteenth-century France and the struggle of parliamentarians to preserve the State and the traditional legal and cultural values that had gone into preserving it as a unique *Monarche de marque*.

In *Etienne Pasquier on Ethics and History*, published by Peter Lang Publishing, in 2007, I give a more complete overview of Pasquier's life from a more traditional methodology, and I pause over his ideal self-portrait he gives his reader for emulation in his *Correspondence*. I outline his ethical program for which he uses vignettes from history to illustrate his ethical points. In the current book I have borrowed Greenblatt's criteria for self-fashioning and have applied them freely to Pasquier's program of self-construction in his career and in his works. The reader can conclude that his life and his works are interwoven with each other. The *Pourparlers* are three brief works that receive more attention here I believe than they have before, as is the case for Pasquier's Book III of his *Recherches de la France* about France's ecclesiastical establishment. More study, perhaps especially for an English-speaking readership, was desirable, and it is my intention that readers will find that here. Finally it is my hope that Pasquier's reception in posterity will continue to unfold for new generations of readers and scholars of France in the Early Modern period.

· 2 ·
PASQUIER'S SELF-FASHIONING AS THE IDEAL PUBLIC SERVANT

1. Pasquier and the Idea of Self-Fashioning

The theories of Stephen Greenblatt and Lisa Jardine[1] about self-fashioning in the Early Modern period have been well known for some time now, but they can in some aspects serve as a framework for an approach to Etienne Pasquier's construction of his career and his persona. He worked consciously and consistently to construct his image and his place in the hierarchy of the *Parlement*. This goal he pursued as parallel to his other one of instructing the monarchy and the public in how best to preserve traditional law and cultural/ethical values in the latter sixteenth century. Though contemporaries would never have formulated such a term as "self-fashioning," still a modified version of Greenblatt's and Jardine's approach is applicable for exploring just what Pasquier and his peers in the Paris Parliament might have meant as an equivalent to our modern notion of advancement, realizing that the equally modern notion of the "self-made" professional is also anachronistic, when applied to the period. Advancement for contemporaries could in certain aspects come down to what Pasquier wishes for his son, Pierre, who has just received a military promotion. In a letter to Pierre he congratulates him on his good fortune, which will continue to allow him a place among "les gens de bien et d'honneur" (good and honorable people).[2] In addition, Greenblatt points out that the sixteenth century was a period when the individual was particularly circumscribed by received codes of comportment, and that it was relatively unheard of to rise in society without a distinguished *lignage*,[3] though I find this point quite debatable, as we know next to nothing about Pasquier's parents or about his earliest years. In addition, his son Nicolas himself writes about one's capacity to *parvenir* by dint of personal effort and virtue. The facts we do have about Pasquier's early life have been accounted for in the commentaries and editions of his works that I analyze in my chapter about his reception in posterity and in modern critical works.[4] The most thorough account of Pasquier's life in my opinion is given in Giraud's Introduction to the *Interprétation des Institutes de Justinian*. It is not my intention in this chapter simply to repeat those facts or to supply information where there exist *lacunae*, such as in the lack of details we have about his earliest years. Rather I want to explore strategies Pasquier used to construct his public *persona*. For this purpose I will engage in a close reading of selections from his correspondence and some other writings that illustrate key points of his professional and social ascent as well as points where he makes an effort to influence contemporary values. Greenblatt's theory of self-fashioning and Jardine's analysis of methodologies used by Erasmus for this purpose allow us a glimpse of the individual at work as it were, in the process of building his image. For the modern reader this can be more satisfying than simply reading the "authorized" construction, the final artifact resulting from the polishing process engaged in by the author as self-*encomia* or from other works of praise produced by contemporaries on his behalf.

I have shown Pasquier's efforts to supply such an idealized image of himself especially in certain letters to his friend and colleague, Pierre Pithou, and to his sons Theodore and Pierre,[5] written in the rhetorical vein of the *portrait moral*, and also the idealized self-portrait for emulation as discussed by Michel Beaujour.[6] As Beaujour explains, this is not a continuous narrative, much less an autobiography in any traditional sense, but rather a brief "study" or *récit*, a theme that is in discontinuity with the rest of an author's narrative.[7] This is the case of the letters I have just referenced from Pasquier's published *Correspondence*.

Certainly, the idealized self-portrait as contained in Pasquier's letters, especially that addressed to Pithou, is quite similar to a concept like self-fashioning in the Early Modern period as theorized by Greenblatt. Pasquier decribes for Pithou fundamentals of his life's itinerary, largely along thematic lines, partly for the sake of giving *exempla* for emulation, without an explicit care for chronological order, except to refer to his "youth," his beginnings at the *palais*, or his more mature years. His treatment of his activities by theme suggests that he had always been consciously building his career, according to certain specific ideals, honoring traditions, boundaries and other norms of the parliamentary *milieu*. Greenblatt cites Clifford Geertz, who affirms that if books and letters are "cultural artifacts," "so are humans themselves." This point can be seen as part of the interest in reading Pasquier today, since his work is indeed an artifact in Geertz's sense, and a rich one that introduces us to the whole spectrum of literary, political, religious and philosophical life in France in the second half of the sixteenth century, with serious regard for its roots in ancient Roman institutions and in medieval French society. To read Pasquier's work is to revisit classical and medieval authors, as well as Montaigne, Marot, the Pléïade and Rabelais. He wants to be a spokesman for these literary and other cultural traditions which he sees as ancillary to the judicial structures that give moorings to the realm, in his own time and for *posterité*. I believe then that Pasquier's itinerary, especially as we see him following received codes of conduct, lends itself to an application of the self-fashioning theory, and perhaps in thinking about Pasquier's self-fashioning it will be most useful to cite some key points of Greenblatt's methodology from his text:

> "There is no such thing as a human nature independent of culture," Geertz writes, meaning by culture not primarily "complexes of concrete behavior patterns—customs, usages, traditions, habit clusters"—"but rather, a set of control mechanisms—plans, recipes, rules, instructions . . . for the governing of behavior."[8]
>
> Self-fashioning is in effect the Renaissance version of these control mechanisms, the cultural system of meanings that creates specific individuals by governing the passage from abstract potential to concrete historical embodiment. Literature functions within this system in three interlocking ways: as a manifestation of the concrete *behavior* of its particular author, as itself the expression of the *codes* by which behavior is shaped, and as a *reflection* upon those codes.[9] (Italics mine)

Thus Greenblatt underlines a self-fashioning that involves all three concepts I have italicized above, that is, the individual's behavior, the codes he or she follows in the act of becoming, and an interpretation or an act of adapting within one's social context. A study of behavior alone, Greenblatt explains, would result in traditional biography. To consider codes or interpretation alone would seem to reduce to ideological analysis or to compartmentalize detail into "historical background" without due regard for contextualization of particular individuals, places, or institutions.

2. The Stoical Garden: Early Goals and Sensibilities Remembered in Pasquier's Later Correspondence

Although we have little detailed information about Pasquier's early life it is generally noted that he was the first to bring public distinction to his family. Yet it would seem clear that his decisions to study at the Paris College de Presle (where he was aware of, and perhaps met Ramus) as well as at the great law faculty of Toulouse, then in (Italy) had to be directed by his father or by some other guardian figure who was conscious of the fact that legal training was the principal means by which most young men of Pasquier's social milieu could achieve professional success. His family thus acknowledged the eminence of the law profession, and as a young student at Presle and later, Pasquier consciously applied himself to following the expected behaviors and learned the codes of the legal class which he interpreted on his way to rise in eminence, as a king's counselor and as a president of the *Cours des Comptes*. There is much evidence that would allow us to conclude that Pasquier and Pierre Pithou worked together on projects of law or erudition. His letter[10] to him which I have mentioned and to which I here draw the reader's attention once again is autobiographical in character and although it dates from 1582–83 when Pasquier was already 54 years of age, it suggests habits of cultivating good mental hygiene and considerable personal organization that the two students must have learned during their earliest schooling, and which he asserts he applied upon arrival at the Paris *Parlement*:

> "Ce mot de jardin me fait ressouvenir quelle fust ma première déliberation lorsque j'arrivay au Palais, car tout ainsy que nous diversifions nos jardins, de ce costé-là d'un parterre et compartiment de fleurs souëfves et odoriferantes, icy d'un plant d'arbres qui rapportent des fruicts, là d'une potagerie qui regarde la necessité du mesnage, meslans par ce moyen le plaisir avec le profit, aussi ay-je voulu mesnager mes actions, tanstost en ce qui appartenoit à la necessité de mon estat, pour subvenir à moi et aux miens, tantost d'estude serieuse, puis de joyeuse, me jouant diversement de mon esprit, sans que le plaisir m'ait jamais faict mettre en oubly ce qui estoit de mon estat, ni que l'exercise de mon estat m'ait faict oublier rien du contentement que je prens de ces gentillesses et gaillardises d'esprit."[11] (The word "garden" puts me in mind of when I began (my career) at the Courts, since, just as we vary and classify our gardens—here a bed of sweet, highly fragrant flowers; still further, an orchard for fruit trees and still further a field for growing vegetables needed for household cooking—with pleasure and profit thus blended together as it were. I wanted to manage my activities in a

> similar way, in what touched on the necessities of my circumstances in life, especially the need to care for my family and me. In the same way I cultivated a variety of studies, some serious, required by my work, and others less pressing, more enjoyable, since my mind required variety upon which to focus. At the same time, these pleasurable pursuits never made me forget my duties, nor did duty cause me to forget the welcome refreshment I received from such agreeable and challenging exercises for the mind. (My translation)

In his on-going, deliberate constructing of his image as a *zélateur du bien public*, promoting and preserving traditional values, Pasquier invokes a stoic metaphor of gardens. As each sort of garden (*à fleurs* (flower garden), orchards and *potager* (for vegetables)) is arranged aesthetically but also functionally to correspond to the duties and practical needs of life, Pasquier suggests that the mind should be as well organized, developed and nurtured as are traditional French *parterres*, orchards and kitchen gardens, from which one can draw what is necessary for two kinds of nurture, that is, both for the serious business of living and making a profit, and the equally necessary time for intellectual and social stimulation (*plaisir*, symbolized here by the esthetic appeal of the *parterre à fleurs*). In addition, the very nature of "relaxation" for Pasquier, Pithou and others of the judicial circle had very definite characteristics, linked to traditional classical and Christian injunctions against wasting time, and which Pasquier and his circle seemed to have followed. It could scarcely ever have meant "doing nothing," or the purely passive activities that in part characterize some entertainments in our own day.

3. Diversions and Salon Life in the Service of Pasquier's Construction of Self

Emma Cayley[12] analyses the development of pastime games played by both sexes together throughout the Middle Ages, many of which survived intact or in variation in the late sixteenth century. Pasquier was also fond of games that involved mental acumen, some of which he discusses in Book IV of his *Recherches de la France*.[13] The reader familiar with Pasquier's biography recalls the salon *divertissements* he engaged in with fellow jurists, including Loisel and Pithou, as well as such poet notables as Nicolas Rapin, at the salon of the Des Roches, mother and daughter, during the *Grands Jours* at Poitiers in 1579.[14] A flea that appeared on the bosom of Catherine Des Roches became the object of a sort of poetic competition among poetically inclined friends, with epigrams written in French, Latin and Greek, and in which Pasquier's own poetical works played a prominent role. He skillfully plays the gallant in his sparring match in verse with the equally adept Catherine Des Roches. He later had the *recueil* published, and he included in that edition a print of the well-known portrait of him by De Hoey, done much later, at Troyes, and to which we shall return. Thus in the above-cited excerpt from Pasquier's letter to Pithou, as in the episode of the *Puce*, Pasquier carefully edits and constructs the image he wishes his readers, both his colleagues and the public, to have of him. In the published editions of *La Puce*, it is probable that he worked with the editors to arrange the text to ensure for himself a central role in the esteem of his circle of prominent judicial and poet colleagues. In addition, in the text of his letter to Pithou, he wishes to be seen as a man of balance and cultivation who appreciates beauty and the joys of mental acumen and intellectual challenge, which he finds restorative. Above all he wishes to personify the statesman, the man of duty whose services and advice are preeminently sought after by great and small alike. This desire to be known for superlative judgment is exemplified further in the balance he maps out in his metaphor of the varieties of gardens. The episode of the *Puce* showcases him as a lively companion and *un homme d'esprit*, who is already an established poet among peers. Thus he is careful to follow the social codes of his judicial class. In a similar vein to that of the *Puce*, we shall return to a discussion of another vehicle of Pasquier's self-fashioning, the poetic sparring around the "handless" De Hoey portrait of him that resulted in his publishing another collection of poems, this time on the theme of *La Main de Pasquier*. That collective effort focuses on the "hands" or invisibility thereof, of their subject. We shall discuss these themes, but first a return to the letter to Pierre Pithou.

4. "Making Books" and Petrarcan Imitation for Mental Hygiene as a Lasting Testimony of Pasquier's Character

Pasquier shares with Pithou his early excitement about the benefits of reading and writing. He approaches the question of *oisiveté*, an ambivalent term during the Renaissance and one difficult to define, in reference to his forced convalescence away from the law courts due to mushroom poisoning, an episode he also alludes to in his *Pourparler du prince*, and which served as the pretext for the dialogic exchanges contained in that text. Pasquier explains that he is not by nature *oiseux*, which in this context we may perhaps assume to mean idle or lazy, albeit another contemporary meaning, that used by Montaigne, indicated the employing of one's leisure time (*loisirs*) in preparing for some task, event or other activity.[15] This definition then, might logically apply to Pasquier's activity if his use of the term *oiseux* did not have so clearly the more modern meaning of idleness, given the strict context of the sentence. It remains, however, and Pasquier underlines it in this letter, that his *loisirs* or leisure time pursuits—"making books," poetic composition, games of acumen or "lighter" reading and writing, and *not* preparing law briefs—entirely complemented and prepared him for his official tasks as an ambitious and distinguished parliamentarian who would also be counselor to four kings of France. Although ultimately, as an elder statesman who had carefully cultivated a reputation for *gravitas*, he debated within himself, and predictably, shared in his correspondence, whether to edit out his early love poetry and similar works such as his pastoral work, *Le Monophile*. He explains to Pithou that he "made books" (*je me mis a faires des livres*) "in conformity with his (young) age, and with the naiveté and sincerity of heart that he then wore on his sleeve" (mes des livres conformes à mon aage et a l'honneste liberté que je portois sur le front).[16] He has decided to let the public see him as a once young, Ronsardian lover. The extent to which the young Pasquier ever invested time with the ordinary pleasures of young friends, athletics, the hunt, or the like, or romantic involvements is unknown to us.[17] He adopted the Petrarchan sonnet among other forms, in imitation of Ronsard and the Pléïade with whom he was on familiar terms. His verse can seem too derivative, his Petrarchan "passion" more of an exercise than a reflection of much real sentiment. If Tyard "Laura" was "Pasithée," Pasquier's own was "Sabina," and he, a married man, prudently lets us know that she is his "maistresse *fictive*."[18]

5. "Le Service des dames," and Pasquier's Professional Advancement

We shall return to what Pasquier has to say about managing a married relationship, and also his own marriage. He married a rather wealthy former client, a widow, albeit a young one, with whom he had six children and for whom he had won a case, Françoise Belen. This relationship can appear not so much a love match as a satisfactory legal arrangement. She was grateful to him for winning her case for her. He mentions no head-long and passionate meeting of hearts. We know that the same contract approach characterized the experience of other humanists, such as More, and of patrician marriages in general in the Early Modern period. In addition, for his advancement, Pasquier knew that he needed a stable domestic foyer with a predictable and presentable spouse. Pasquier has much to say about how a man may have a happy marriage, though in his letter to Jean Le Picard he avows that he may be out of his depth: "J'en parle comme un aveugle des couleurs" (I sound like a blind man, trying to describe color). This may be simply a rhetorical disavowal since in fact he has much to say about women, and primarily about how a man may make his way in the world by maintaining good relationships with them. He appears to respect women and their dignity within a marriage:

> Je sçay bien que la femme se doit rendre souple aux volontez de son mary, mais aussi un marry par prerogative de son sexe se veuille roidir contre toutes les opinions de sa femme, il perd tout. *Car si la femme n'avoit ce privilege de desdire parfois les opinions de son mary, elle ne penserait avoir sa condition différente d'avec celle des servants*. Je seray plus hardi et diray qu'encore vaut-il mieux ployer sous une femme testue en choses specialement indifférentes que vivre en perpetuelle inquietude d'esprit. (I know that the woman should give in easily to her husband's wishes, but if a husband, thinking it his male prerogative to gainsay all his wife's opinions, then he will lose everything. If a woman does not feel that she has the right to disagree occasionally with her husband, then there is little reason for her to feel that he regards her as more than just another female servant. I will be even more daring and suppose that it is far better to give in to the wishes of a stubborn wife, especially in small matters, than to live with constant unpleasantness between you.) (my translation)

When Pasquier notes that the wife should give in rather readily to her husband's wishes, and that a husband should be reasonable and accommodating to his wife, he echos the Pauline instruction about husbands and wives in Ephesians 5, which calls for mutual respect and love between the spouses. In Ephesians, and also in other sections of the letter to Le Picard, we see that Pasquier really does prefer marriage for himself over celibacy, and that he does have a fondness for conjugal life. He explains that he is not interested in debating the virtues of these two states of life, as this has been done by others and has become a rhetorical commonplace.[19] Marriage favors the social stability needed to promote "le bien public." Moreover, a life without women is unthinkable: "We no longer relate to women only when we no longer relate at all," he tells Le Picard. While he seems always to refer to women as the "the other," as opposed to "we," *the "reality" of men*, he also demonstrates what may be appreciated as a sincere concern for what may arguably be termed, at the risk of anachronism, "women's rights," and for "feminine psychology" *avant la lettre*. But, as we noted above, he is also conscious that peace and stability at home are a basis of a husband's successful public career: "Et je vous respond en un mot que c'est apporter grand repos à son esprit quand on vit en repos avec sa femme."[20] He also notes quite frankly, and significantly for us, in another letter, this time addressed to Guillaume de Marillac[21] that "le service des dames" is an involvement he gives himself to happily, "body and spirit." Harmonious relationships with prominent women are a *sine qua non* of success in public life:

> Je veux doncques en ceste estrif conclurre que tant s'en faut que pour parvenir aux honneurs, ce soit chose mal compatible d'estre serviteur des femmes, qu'à l'opposite je pense que leur service est accident inseparable de ceux qui veulent parvenir. Car mesme, si nous voulons peser plus subtilement les choses (mais toutefois à leur vray poinct), vous trouverez que ceux qui montent aux estats ou par vertu, ou par pecune, ou par leur diligence, ou par leur dexterité et industrie, ou par importunitez et prière, ou par faveur, ou par piperie encore, sont en ceci toutes leurs actions accompagnees du feminin.[22] (I would like then in this (*place-estrif*) to conclude that although the ambition for honors may seem incompatible with 'the service of women,' I say that quite the opposite is true. Ingratiating oneself with women is an indispensable component for those who wish to succeed. Moreover, if we want to weigh matters more subtly, but at the same time, at their just measure, you will find that those who rise to high estate, whether because of their virtue, or by means of money, or their diligence, their dexterity and industry, or by seeking favors, and prayer, by who they know or by fraud itself, all of their ambitions and actions are accompanied by a woman's influence.) (My translation)

This text could be taken for a citation from Balzac's *Père Goriot*. With enjoyment and idealistic admiration, but also mixed with cynicism and suggestions of misogeny, not to mention misanthropy,[23] Pasquier calculates what is necessary for political and social ascent, his, and that of others, as an ordinary rule. We wonder to what extent he "gave himself body and soul" to get to know certain powerful women who could advance him; for example, one can speculate as to what level of intimacy he attained with another of his eminent female correspondents, the Maréchale de Retz.[24]

6. Poetry and Pasquier's Tribute to Celebrated Ladies

Pasquier also gave credit to a number of other women of political ascendancy in French history and in contemporary times, notably, the queen mother, Catherine de Médicis, who he very much admired and respected, no doubt, always from a distance, in his context of parliamentarian and royal advisor. He regards Catherine as having been a decisive and wise stateswoman, whose interventions were helpful in curtailing the bloodshed of the Wars of Religion. Pasquier admired this strong and resourceful woman, this "très sage princesse"[25] who also engaged in self-construction as she gained prominence after the untimely and tragic death in a jousting accident of her husband, Henri II. She calculated the most prudent, personally useful moment for her appearance on the political stage, and steered the country through the Wars of Religion, seeking pacification through her ministers, L'Hospital, Pasquier and their parliamentarian colleagues, and successfully relaxing rigor, momentarily, for "ceux de la Religion." Pasquier also devotes a chapter of Book II of his *Recherches de la France* to such wise queen mothers as Catherine, who as regents protected their sons' interests during their minorities, a circumstance that Pasquier finds particularly precarious for a state given the potential for sedition by ambitious princes.[26] After his encomium of Blanche of Castille, mother of Saint Louis (IX) and regent during his minority, Pasquier reserves *hyperdulia* for Catherine, as seen in this epitaph:

"Cy gist la fleur de l'estat de Florence." ("Here lies the flower of the City-state of Florence.")
Veufve de Roy, mere de Roy aussi, (A king's widow, and mother of king(s) also,)
Qui conserva, d'un merveilleux soucy (Who guarded with a wonderful care)
Tous ces enfans contre la violence (all of her children against violence)
Le ciel permet que par un coup de lance, (Heaven allowed that by a thrust of the lance.)
Nostre soleil fut du tout obscurcy (Our sun was darkened)
Nous allumast les feus dedans la France (It *lit* fires throughout France)

Mais ceste Dame aimée d'un haut Coeur (but that beloved, good hearted lady)
I'arant aux coups de la haine et rancoeur, (confronting hatred and rancor,)
Seule fermait à nos troubles la porte. ([She] alone barred the gates against our troubles.)
Enfin est morte une veille de Rois, (Finally she passed from us, (this) forerunner of kings,)
Et par sa mort je crain, peuple François, (And by her death I fear, people of France,)
Qu'aveq'la paix, la Roiauté soit morte. (Both peace and the monarchy may have perished.)[27]

Pasquier tried his hand at all of the poetic genres, both the "historic" forms such as epitaphs and love verse. It is always debatable to what extent sixteenth-century poetry reflects the true affective erotic life of the poet. This is true also of Pasquier's love verse, which he composed partly as one of his strategies of social ascent. We know that his fellow jurists wrote poetry and frequented poets. In his efforts to compose amorous verse, he declares to Pithou that he does not believe he has been guilty of "folie," any more than such could be said of:

> . . . ce grand Petrarque et Bembe italiens, et entre les nostres Ronsard, Bellay et infinité d'autres gens de nom. Au contraire, je me poursuade d'estre, d'icy en avant, compté pour le huictiesme sage. Car il est certain que Solon, ce grand législateur d'Athènes que l'on met entre les sept sages de Grèce, escrivit livres d'amourettes en vers, et après luy ce grand philosophe Platon, en prose, avec lesquels j'aimeray mieux estre mis au rang des fols que estre en opinion de sage au milieu de la populace.[28] (. . . the great Italian authors Petrarch and Bembo, and among our own, Ronsard and Du Bellay and a vast number of other distinguished names. On the contrary, I believe I shall be named as the eighth sage. Since it is certain that Solon, that great Athenian legislator who was one of the seven sages of Greece, wrote collections of amorous verse, and after him, the great philosopher Plato, in prose, with whom I would rather be associated—with such "fools" than to be considered wise among the run of commoners.) (My translation)

Thus Pasquier does not blush to associate himself with the most illustrious of Italian poets first, and we know that while he had a familiarity with Italian language and culture from his early Italian schooling, as well as a genuine admiration for the Italian vernacular and its poetry, he, a Frenchman asserts his own poetic superiority, and makes a metonymical use of his own name and reputation to assert the superiority of French verse in general, in comparison with that of Italy's greatest masters. He describes for Pithou his daily dedication to practicing verse, "writing epigrams in bed at night, "une ou deux heures la nuit" (one or two hours a night), when his full day of legal writings and consultations was over. Pasquier is self-congratulatory on his superiority as a poet. He asserts that his poet-parliamentarian colleague, Thomas Sebillet, whom we know for his *art poétique*, had encouraged his poetic efforts. We remember too, that he boldly declares in Book VII of his *Recherches de la France* that the sonnet form was not Petrarcan but Provençal, and we know that Pasquier counts these latter poets as French. Thus Pasquier styles himself as a spokesman to his readers both contemporary and future for the superiority of French *lettres*, even over those of Classical Rome and *Quattrocento* Italy. Through his published *Correspondence* Pasquier weaves his public *persona* as a man of letters, a literary critic and also a historian and ethicist whose great monument to his country, and also to himself, is the continuous project of his *Recherches de la France*. He had many reasons to dedicate the first book of his *Recherches* to a prominent patron of *lettres*, the Cardinal de Lorraine.[29]

7. The Cardinal de Lorraine

Pasquier's first letter of the second book of his correspondence[30] is written to "Monsieur l'illustrissime et reverendissime Charles, Cardinal de Lorraine." He duly humbles himself in noting that he ought decently to remain silent and not trouble the great man by offering him a copy of "ces miennes petites Recherches." He recognizes that the cardinal is owed "foy et homage" by "chacun", and, very significantly, for his own goal of self-fashioning, he uses the *topos* of France as a vast "théâtre"; he has also used this same *topos* in the introduction to his *Recherches*, in application to the king's own position with regard to his subjects. Just as he explains in this same text that the "eyes of all" are watching and imitating the king's most intimate movements, and by extention, in this letter, the Cardinal's, since he has been constituted by the king as "souverain après luy." From this we can surmise that through his association in print with the great, Pasquier would like the focus of attention, admiration and emulation to be on himself also. He follows strategies and rhetorical codes similar to those that Guillaume Budé had used when offering his own *apophtègmes* to François I, and which we note in any illustration of a king or another great personnage being offered a book by its author, who hopes to bask in the great person's prestige. Pasquier remembers that many have offered Charles "antiquaillies de marque" that now grace his "maisons de parade." He teases out the association between the Cardinal's taste for *antiquailles* and his own "fragments des *anciennetez* de nostre France," which he now sends him. He announces his hopes and ambition: if the Cardinal will but show his book some passing attention, Pasquier hopes to enjoy greater success by this than have other authors:

> Je me promets avoir la fortune de tant plus favorable que la plupart de ceux qui ont par le passé employé leur entendement à escrire. . . . . . j'ay rappellé en ce lieu toute mon estude et labeur en la deduction de la France, principal but de tous vos discours et pensées. (I am confident to have much greater success than most of the others who in the past undertook to put pen to paper. . . . I have recalled here all my study and labor in the understanding of France (and her experience) which is equally the object of all your own speeches and reflexions.) (My translation)

The cardinal's favor will help Pasquier gain renown for his writings about France and especially her well-being, which as he indicates, has always been the cardinal's own concern, not only as a patron of culture and values but as a pillar of both secular and ecclesiastical law as a prince of the Church and a close minister of the king and of Catherine de Medicis. In Charles de Lorraine, then, Pasquier sees a personification of the values that he wishes to preserve in French life and for the defense of which he too wishes to gain renown, serving as what he calls a *chevalier de la plume* (a knight brandishing a pen) in this instance through writing his *Recherches*, which he strategically offers for the approbation of none other than France's chief prelate.[31]

We know that the first publication of the *Recherches de la France* in 1560 did indeed accrue to its author the beginnings of that renown that he sought through the associations we have mentioned, and through many others. He gained eminence in circles of letters and also among his judicial peers. Let me return us briefly to the letter to Pithou, in which he tells his readers through this worthy old friend about the superior rank he has achieved among his legal peers: "Le temps, peu a peu, m'appresta tel lieu et advancement entre mes compagnons que je puis maintenant tenir." ("With time I rose in the ranks of my companions to the place I now hold.")[32]

8. Pasquier's Relationship with Fellow Jurist-Poets and with the Dames Des Roches

He also knew how to ingratiate himself with other jurists for whom the writing of verse was also a pastime and a hallmark of their station as "gens de marque," as Pasquier referred to them, while including himself at their level of distinction.[33] In 1579 he had been sent to preside at the *Grands Jours* in Poitiers, where he also joined in the salon life of the Des Roches, Madeleine and Catherine, mother and daughter, and where he had collaborated with his fellow jurists on the *Poème de la puce*. This had been an opportunity for him to demonstrate the prominence he enjoyed among his peers that we just saw he described to Pithou, who himself was among the contributors of verse, both to *la Puce*, and to another collective work, *La Main de Pasquier*, occasioned this time by another session of the *Grands Jours*, this time at Troyes, in 1583. It was during this stay in Troyes that Pasquier had his portrait painted by the painter Jean de Hoey. Lisa Jardine, writing about Erasmus[34] and others, has pointed out the special significance of visual depiction in the construction of a desired image.

The portrait depicts Pasquier at age 65, still relatively thin, wearing a small beard and dressed in a large, plain collar and a button-down black vest. Over this he wears in open fashion the majestic black robes of his office, as well as the black bonnet, another significant symbol of his station. Thus he wears the official costume of a parliamentarian. His vesture and expression produce the desired effect of *gravitas*. A contemporary controversy in which lawyers had been required to reveal their compensation is said to have been the reason why Pasquier's hands are not depicted. Around the lozenge-shaped portrait reads the inscription: "Nulla hic Paschasio manus est, lex Cincia quipped Caussidicos nullas sanxit habere manus." Here, Pasquier has no hands; as Cincius wishes advocates to spend their lives without them." (My translation.) He seems to have liked the over-all effect of this portrait since another, accompanying a 1633 edition of his *Recherches de la France*,[35] gives an almost identical rendering with the same inscription, though this canvas is squared rather than in lozenge form. The inscription about Cincius and "hands" seems to have served Pasquier's keen sense of judicial ethics, which we know he shared in a famous letter to his son Theodore about the duties of his legal profession.[36] Before we discuss the relevance of the De Hoey portrait to the collective poem *La main de Pasquier*, a bit more ought to be said about his portrait as compared to those of others in the period. Pasquier's parliamentarian colleague, fellow antiquarian and collaborator in writing projects, Claude Faucet, had a very similar portrait made of himself which accompanies a posthumous edition of his works from 1610. The portrait is lozenge form, again with an inscription, though this says only "Claudii Falchetii Franciar. Antiquitat. Scrip. Aetatis Anno LXX. Sal. M.D. LXXXXIX." (Claude Faucet, author of the Antiquities of France, age 70, in the year of grace 1599.) The lozenge is inserted within a rectangle. Below the portrait are Fauchet's heraldic arms, with the legend: "ce qui estoit espars et delaissé ha ce Faucet aux François amassé." (What was scattered and neglected this Fauchet has collected (restored) for the French people.) (My translation). Fauchet's portrait is without the bonnet but features the same robes and the same flowing beard as the picture of the older Pasquier from the edition of 1633 just described. There is the same aspect of *gravitas*. It is perhaps an interesting aside to note that we have no real evidence that these paintings depict the subject's actual appearance. Philippe Desan has pointed out in his recent study of portraits of Montaigne that an artist sought not so much to depict the subject in faithful detail as to reproduce a "type," and that is why, Desan explains, so many Early Modern portraits look so similar to each other.[37] The portraits of Montaigne relay the same virtues as those successfully portrayed in those of Pasquier and Fauchet, and Montaigne is often portrayed in somber dress in contemporary portraits. In other pictures he wears brighter, more courtly clothing such as in the case of the so-called "Versailles" portrait where he appears in the costume of the mayor of Bordeaux. I am unaware of any such "courtly" depictions of Pasquier, or of Fauchet, for that matter, and the only group "portrait" of Pasquier is provided not on canvas but in pen and ink in the written depiction of his exchanges with his peers that I have already analyzed, Loisel's *Pasquier ou dialogue des avocats*.[38] But we can see that according to Greenblatt's criteria, associates can help in the individual's quest of self-fashioning, and Loisel has certainly done that for Pasquier, in his *Dialogue*. But it bears continued comment that, as in the case of the portraits of Pasquier as well as in the one of Fauchet discussed above and the contemporary portraits we have of Montaigne, there is no display of the subject's hands, with some exceptions in the case of the author of the *Essais*. One contemporary picture shows him touching his great chain of the Order of St. Michel, while in another he is kneeling with hands joined in prayer. Seventeenth-century portraits sometimes show him holding his book of the *Essais*.[39] But again, as Desan points out, a portrait is often an ideological investment,[40] which brings us back to De Hoey's "handless" Pasquier, which we can assume to be an investment of the latter's desire to personify iconic lawyerly honesty and parliamentary virtue. In the salon life at Troyes during the *Grands Jours*, with the recent controversy over the appropriateness of disclosure of lawyers' compensation that we have mentioned, together with the appearance of Pasquier's "handless" portrait, *La main* became a focus of another collective poetical work by Pasquier and his colleagues and admirers, among them Pithou and Loisel as well as the eminent Achille du Harlay. Pasquier directed, edited and published this collection, a series of poems on the theme of *la main*, in which the emphasis was on the central significance of his *writings* on French law, history, poetry and culture, hence the helpful synechdoche of the hands, with reference to verse from his "hand," or his "pen." Thus De Hoey's portrait as well as the poetical collective tribute it inspired was directed and intended by Pasquier to put his name forward, and *la main* was also discussed by Loisel in his own encomium of his friend, *Pasquier ou dialogue des avocats*, in which Pasquier is seen to interact with his legal colleagues as their moral center. Loisel thus also helped him to construct his career and his public image.

Antoine Loisel had become eminent in his own right, and Pasquier takes pride in their life-long friendship. They had attended the Collège de Presle, where Ramus was an instructor. However debatable Pasquier's own claim, in his correspondence, to have known Ramus well (or at all, on personal terms),[41] we know that Loisel did have a personal relationship with the *lecteur royal*, who named him his executor. Of course he, like Pasquier and all of their parliamentarian colleagues, was conscious of trying to achieve prominence. Although he had initially shown interest in a medical career, his father persuaded him to choose law: a doctor, though he enjoys respect, always remains (just) a doctor, but a lawyer can rise to be a *président ou chancelier*, he told him. Loisel had become a friend and a close working associate with another of their famous professors, Jacques Cujas. At Bourges, Pierre Pithou joined them, and the three worked in a library after dinner evenings, often until three in the morning. Loisel played important political roles. When the duke of Alençon was to marry Elizabeth I, Loisel examined the wedding contract and advised against the marriage, since the provisions were not favorable to France. Like Pasquier's colleagues Claude Fauchet and Pierre Pithou, Loisel was also an antiquarian, and he published a study of the antiquities of Pontoise.[42] Loisel, then, a boyhood friend, was now a well-established personage in the view of both the royal family and his parliamentarian colleagues, known for his judgment and *gravitas*, and it is to him that Pasquier addresses the first letter of his published correspondence, in which he discusses his own epistolary project as on a par with those of *les gens de marque* in the history of epistolary authorship, for example, Cicero or Pliny the Younger. Thus once again we see that he places himself tacitly among the great. But he is not as openly bold in asserting his epistolary abilities; rather he uses a rhetorical *topos*, an almost mandatory stylistic device for writers of the period, of his unworthiness for such a project. He constructs his claim of his unworthiness: he will pursue the daunting project, he allows, because his friend Loisel has coaxed him into it. Having accepted the task, he willingly "passes the bounds of all shame," and accepts to "blush" at whatever criticism may come his way. But even here he turns the image to his own credit! We must make no mistake, he sees himself as an intrepid pioneer in the epistolary genre. If others more able than he will come later to such a project, Pasquier is the first! He will be the one who "face planche aux plus sages" (serve as a gangplank that others, better than he, may board the ship).[43]

9. Constructing His Image as Defender of the State Against Invented Enemies

Pasquier's eagerness to associate himself and his career with Loisel is an example of his desire to build his reputation and achieve by means of a legal career, the "highest honors" available to an individual in the kingdom of France.

We have just seen that Loisel's father wished this same success for him, and Pasquier himself suggests that such a path would inevitably orient one to the most respectable, coveted goals, ones that always helped not only one's own situation in life but also that of others. One could serve, to the general admiration, as a *zélateur du bien public*.[44] As we continue to follow, at the risk of anachronism, Greenblatt's template of self-fashioning, we note his observation that the individual wishing to construct his name usually had confronted an important adversary, whose defeat helped him to prove his mettle. Pasquier found such "adversaries" to defeat, in certain legal cases he argued, the briefs which he was careful to include later in his published works. In the case of the Sieur d'Arconville, he demonstrates his successful concern for courtroom ethics and for a fair trial for the accused. He explains that d'Arconville, a young nobleman accused of multiple murders, was paraded through the streets and into open court on a cart, loaded down with chains, a traditional means of demonstrating to the public the accused prisoner's heinous criminality, and which in effect already tried and condemned him in public opinion.[45] Pasquier took pride in himself as a shrewd judge of character. He intuited d'Arconville's innocence simply by noting the composure he saw in his expression, as he explains in his correspondence. He single-handedly shouted down the angry mob in court, and got d'Arconville acquitted. Thus by innate intuition as well as uncommon oratory, he "defeated" the injustice and sensationalism that could attend a controversial case, and he allowed cool-headedness and justice to prevail. This case gained Pasquier a great deal of attention. He records its import for his career in his correspondence.[46]

Of course the Jesuit case is the best known and the one which follows Greenblatt's template for conflict with an "adversary." Pasquier was asked to defend the University of Paris against the Jesuits' desire to teach under its aegis, awarding their own degrees. This case and the publicity it was provided proved to be decisive for Pasquier's social and professional ascent. I think it worth considering that, whatever Pasquier's personal reaction to the Jesuits, whose "threat" to the State he essentially invents to meet the Parliament's and his own self-interest, it was clearly a most useful strategy in terms of his professional rise, to adopt an anti-Jesuit stance. The construction of an "enemy" permitted Pasquier to be seen to ride to the defense of the whole nation. The *contrived* quality of his hostility to the relatively new order also appears plausible since Pierre Pithou, himself a Protestant, admired the Jesuits as "auxiliaries de bonnes études." Moreover, the Jesuits had been well received by French Catholic bishops, including Pasquier's own patron, the cardinal de Lorraine, who ceded to them the Collège de Clermont, as well as by rank and file Catholics throughout the kingdom, for the noted quality of their preaching, their pedagogy among the young and their pastoral ministry to the sick, and the like.[47] Only the University of Paris and Parliament opposed them, invoking the Gallican tradition, which in principle was a safeguard against ultramontaine ideas and interventions. It was imperative for the success of Pasquier's ambitions, as a young lawyer, that he be seen to side with the University and with his fellow parliamentarians. It was the Gallican principle that widened the stage as it were, and allowed him to escalate the Jesuit case from simply a representing of the University's complaint, reframing it as an urgent matter of national security.[48] Pasquier had his brief of the Jesuit case published for the first time in Mettayer and L'Huilier's 1596 edition of his *Recherches*, in Book III, which as we have detailed, is a Gallican interpretation of the history of Christianity which he offers as an instructive parallel for contemporary religio-political conditions. Pasquier's propaganda piece about the Jesuit case appeared as a lengthy chapter of Book III in all subsequent editions of the *Recherches de la France* and is referenced occasionally in his *Correspondence*, and in some of his verse. He amplified further his view (and that of the *Parlement*) of the case's importance in a satirical diatribe, *Le catéchisme des jésuites*, which appeared in regular editions, including international translations from 1602. This work and its wide dissemination, much of which Pasquier oversaw or at least encouraged, now gained him desired international attention, especially in predominantly Protestant countries, England, Holland and the German states.[49] Of course, Pasquier's interpretation of Jesuit motives is very bluntly biased, in a biased age. He dismisses the Jesuits as a "hermaphrodite order" that is, and admittedly unheard of for him and for his time, a sacerdotal congregation comporting itself at once as a religious order and also assuming the offices assigned to parish (secular) priests—a combination of attributes and functions that was not then known in conventional practice. He also referred to them as a "sect," a meretricious term. Jesuits were as dangerous for ecclesiastical and national unity, in Pasquier's mind, as he assessed Calvinism and Lutheranism to be. He uses dramatic rhetoric to call attention to himself as a national hero willing to sound the alarm, heedless of danger or cost to himself. Pasquier thus strategically bypasses the facts that the Jesuits were a legitimate Catholic religious order authorized by bulls of popes Paul III and Julius III, that they had been favorably received in the rest of France and in Europe, and that they were *bona fide* Catholic priests and erudite, serviceable pedagogues. His choice to dramatically defame them serves his project of self-construction. It allows him to "champion" those whose own "rights" could then be cast by him as under potential of threat: the University of Paris, the Gallican Church, his colleagues in Parliament and the king himself. His rhetorical style supposed that a "defeat" of the Jesuits would assure the good of *posterité* and *le bien public*. He saw to it that *France* would be in his debt, ironically, for what his biographer Giraud later characterizes as his "désinteressement." We shall see that his anti-Jesuit campaign went farther than was ultimately good for his own interests, especially in posterity, since Henri IV granted teaching privileges to the order, which gained more significant currency in Parisian society. We know that Jesuit father François Garasse launched his own anti-Pasquier campaign of invective, ironically charging Pasquier with undermining royal authority. And it has been speculated that Nicolas Pasquier, whose success his father did so much to construct, was perhaps impeded in his career when he defended his father, in writing, against criticism by Garasse and certain other members of the order. Very interestingly, the Trévoux Press, influenced by Jesuits, launched the famous 1723 edition of Pasquier's *Oeuvres*, which reprinted not his own defense brief in favor of the University but that of Versoris, the Jesuits' own defense counsel. Perhaps also quite ironically, Pasquier's satire of the Jesuit *Constitutions* and allied documents did much to disseminate in print and by word of mouth the Jesuit world-view to a wide international audience. Having discussed how Pasquier used and to no small degree invented adversaries to discredit in his project of self-construction, we can now turn to ways that he sought to construct, or to fashion, the life and career of his son Nicolas, as he did those of two other sons, Theodore and Pierre. Just as we have seen that the Salon poets at Poitiers and at Troyes as well as Antoine Loisel and others had helped to create Pasquier's own public persona, so he wanted to have his character and achievements reflected in the lives of certain others.

10. Pasquier's Fashioning of His Sons' Careers

I have discussed the letters Pasquier wrote to his two sons, Theodore and Pierre, concerning the conduct that would become them, and also what behavior to avoid in their respective professions of the law and in military leadership.[50] We can feel authorized to assume that their famous father did everything possible to shape the educations as well as the social and professional *entrées* of his sons, also arranging advantageous marriages for them, if the recorded experience of another son, Nicolas is an indication.

Nicolas Pasquier like Theodore followed his father in the magistracy. He inherited Etienne's work habits, his literary style and his humanistic ethos.

Etienne Pasquier was systematically solicitous of Nicolas' education and career success. He secured for him the post of lieutenant-general of the Angoumois, near Cognac, which can account for the extensive knowledge about weapons featured in Nicolas' work, *le gentilhomme*.[51] The elder Pasquier also arranged his marriage to Susanne de Brémond, with whom he had four children before her death. Nicolas then married Louise Mangot, daughter of Claude Mangot, keeper of the Seals, most probably also a connection gained through his father. Thus we can see Pasquier's strategies for constructing or fashioning, if one prefers, the associations and character of his son Nicolas. In *Le Gentilhomme*, under the rubric entitled "noblesse," Nicolas himself is conscious of the need to make a good public impression. For his "gentleman," he emphasizes: "Il faut qu'il donne une bonne Esperance de luy par toutes sortes d'actes genereux." (He must give a good impression by showing great generosity.) He also acknowledges the almost *sine qua non:* "temoigner qu'il vient d'une tige vrayement vertueux, et que par les objects domestiques, il est incité de ce rendre semblableà eux: à la façon des fruicts qui tiennent de la séve de leur branche, et les ruisseaux de la claret de leur fontaine." (To testify that he is the issue of a truly virtuous lineage and as part of that heritage he is compelled to be like them, just as the fruit is a product of the branch, and the stream partalees of the clarity of the fountain.)[52] Nicolas builds on the august reputation of his father. He uses the metaphors of the "stem" or the "shoot" (tige) and the "branches" with their "fruicts" to show his connectedness to the elder Pasquier's qualities, also with special mention of family virtues that he assures his reader he possesses. Nicolas goes on to state that while there is a special "semence," that is, a "seed" or quality instilled within a nobleman or "gentleman," and that it is good when nobility of birth and that of character come together, still one can attain high virtues and a shining reputation for achievement and service to "le bien public" without benefit of noble birth. Thus Nicolas also reflects his father's social and political attitudes in his own writings. Pasquier also recommended Nicolas' book to influential colleagues.

Nicolas wrote when Malherbe, Du Vair and d'Urfé were on the ascent, and the style and tenor of Pasquier senior and the *Pléïade* poets were fading from fashion. This perhaps accounts for the fact that Nicolas' work, *Le Gentilhomme*, and his published correspondence enjoyed only a *succès d'estime* with the reading public. Pasquier in conclusion had constructed a persona for himself that was to survive more through the republication of his works than through a spirit of family continued through the favorable reception of works by his sons. He was also invoked by succeeding regimes who sought ancestors who could be reinvented to serve their own sense of *raison d'état*, as we shall see in our discussion of Pasquier's *Fortune* in posterity.

· 3 ·

LAW, CUSTOM AND THE INDIVIDUAL, REVISITED IN THE *POURPARLERS*

The *pourparler* is a sub-genre of the dialogue form, current in Pasquier's time. It is akin to the *disputatio*,[1] and is one of a variety of forms Pasquier employs to express his Parisian parliamentarian's views as a good *zélateur du bien public*, as he styles himself in his *Recherches de la France*, and in other works. In all of his writings, Pasquier wants to promote and *preserve* the very best of French values, ethics and culture. Pasquier's three very brief and concise works where he uses this term in the title: the *Pourparler du prince*, the *Pourparler de la loy*, and the *Pourparler d'Alexandre* have received very sparse critical attention.[2] The Middle French term, *pourparler*, denotes an *entretien*, a diplomatic conference, or a discussion preliminary to negotiating a treaty. Why did Pasquier feel the need to write these works, and what specifically had to be negotiated in French society at the time of the appearance of the *Pourparler du prince*, in 1560,[3] or that of *La Loy*, or of *Alexandre*, much later, in 1581? A former master of Pasquier's years at the Collège de Presles, now chancellor of France, Michel de l'Hospital gives a vivid picture of the coming *troubles*.[4]

The harsh repression ordered as a result of the Conjuration of Amboise sparked more dissent and unrest, and l'Hospital launched a project to reform the justice system in the summer of 1560. He had called the Assembly of Fountainbleau, 21 August 1560, and the king called for a meeting of the

Estates of Orléans, on which occasion he tried to ensnare princes favorable to the Huguenot reforms. Auguste de Thou informed the king that only Parliament could try a prince of the blood, at which the king, in Pasquier's words, set up his own government in opposition to the norm. Pasquier saw these royal efforts as regrettable: "nouveautez pour exterminer une autre nouveauté sont vrayement les préparatifs d'une calamité générale . . ." (novelties designed to exterminate other novelties are truly the beginnings of a general calamity).[5] L'Hospital found such unrest, criticism and dissent from Parliamentary policies troubling. In his address to the Paris Parliament on 7 September he called for a meeting of the Estates-General and of the Royal Council. L'Hospital was direct. He gave air to many of the points which are well known political and ethical *topoi* that we shall find deployed once again by Pasquier in his *Pourparlers*. He notes that fundamental French political, religious and cultural values were being eroded by *nouveautés*, so decried and warned against by Montaigne,[6] among many others, including Pibrac.[7] At the base of the problem the chancellor saw the self-interest of the "culprit" parties. L'Hospital notes that many concealed their *ambition* under the veil of religion. He also warns that what is done by the leaders is seen by the people. He is critical of some magistrates who incite unrest when their priority should be to keep the peace and the popular good will. Magistrates should give an example of diplomatic, unifying conduct, but many do the contrary, l'Hospital insists. They interpret events and policies badly, including the meeting at Fountainbleau, when bishops and seneschals were sent to their posts to help quell any troubles. Two particular points made here by l'Hospital and upon which Pasquier will also insist are that no permission is given to do simply as one wills, but all are called to maintain the established order of the kingdom. Of course, these tenets are ambient *topoi* of the period, and they were, as we shall see, part and parcel of ancient Roman law inherited and adapted by the judicial machinery of the French monarchy. Our goal in this chapter, after some more notes about l'Hospital is to see how Pasquier himself will apply them in his three *Pourparlers*. The reform of justice is the chancellor's agenda and he declares that any edicts he pronounces are designed for the public good. He warns that some magistrates practice graft or lengthen trials. He wants to discourage irresponsible ambition in judges. He finds it imperative that courts should always prioritize the king's service, not that of local notables who could be notoriously capricious and corrupt. He declares that old ordinances are to be renewed, no doubt in a spirit of valuing continuity of existing good laws, customs and values.

Given these concerns voiced by l'Hospital in his *discours*, with the contents we have just enumerated, we shall see that the chancellor's concerns were shared by his parliamentary colleagues, and that they would inform Pasquier's own writing and publishing agenda. In reality, long before 1560 Pasquier had been writing about the same concerns regarding both *loy* and *foy*, and the various manners in which his contemporaries sought to articulate these public matters. He shares l'Hospital's concern that many are engaging in public argumentation for their own gain and profit. He is eager that the monarch not himself be guilty of such self-interest and so he writes his three fictive *disputationes*, or *pourparlers*. These he fills with historical references intended to mirror conditions in his own time and to suggest remedies to preserve time-honored values. Pasquier explains in his *Correspondence* that as a very young man in 1558 he had unwittingly eaten some poisonous mushrooms which necessitated an extensive recuperation at his country home in Argenteuil. He notes that he was grateful during that period for the company of learned companions, who are found again as the personages mentioned in the beginning of the *Pourparler du prince*. During his period of recuperation he had ample time to discuss, reflect and write his desire to preserve traditional cultural, political and religious values for the good of the kingdom.

1. The *Pourparler du prince*

In the introductory material of the *Pourparler du prince*, Pasquier notes how much he valued his discussions with "les doctes" and the intellectual stimulation that these discussions afforded him. He uses the metaphor of the iron (*acier*), which when rubbed produces "sparks" or new ideas and realizations. He saw that perhaps in the tradition of the University *disputatio*,[8] such "sparks" make "big fires" in the diversity of the opinions exchanged. The interlocutors in the *Pourparler* are four in number: the *Escolier*, the *Curial*, the *Philosophe* and the *Politique*. Pasquier invokes the example of the Perside princes and poses the question as to what constitutes the most desirable form of government for a republic. There follows the naming of the classical categories of monarchical, aristocratic and popular rule. Pasquier admits that he no longer remembers the details of their discussions but that they had agreed that a good king was best. Then the question arose as to whether the scenario of an astute king with limited counselors or a limited king relying on good counselors was preferable. This question of the king's relative dependence on the counsel he receives is a *topos* of books of conduct or mirrors for princes and a theme to which Pasquier will often return in his *Recherches de la France* and in other writings: for him, a king's minority or manifest mental incapacity are times when government can fall to the ambition of corrupt counselors. He readily recalls the intrigues that surrounded Charles VI in his incapacity as princes of the blood competed for control. Pasquier uses this episode as a historical parallel with the contemporary situation of the vulnerable young Valois ruler at the untimely death, in a jousting accident, of Henri II, 10 June, 1559, and of which Pasquier claims to have been an eye-witness.[9] Unlike his esteemed parliamentarian colleague, the distinguished Jean Du Tillet,[10] Pasquier opposed the ambitions of older royal princes and successfully championed the bid for the regency put forward by the strong-willed Catherine de Médicis, the queen mother, whom Pasquier admired.[11] Pasquier thus obviated a rule by self-serving princes or oligarchies, which he felt would lead to political instability, vulnerability to foreign enemies, and unmanageable popular unrest. In the *Pourparlers*, he gives his views about the best forms of government.

The company in the *Pourparler du prince* debate the question, from Plato's *Republic*, about whether the king should philosophize or whether a philosopher should be king. Pasquier tells us that each of his interlocutors explained his point of view, a pedagogical format to instruct the reader, or listener, to Pasquier's work which typifies this academic *disputatio* genre. Another *leitmotif* that is dominant in his works, as we see here, is that he recognizes the necessity of a *written record* as opposed to oral tradition only, in the passing on of values.[12] After a brief comment by the *Curial* (or courtier)[13] defending the respect due to those of his rank, especially given their oath of loyalty to the king, the *Politic* evaluates a philosophical approach to kingship of which he ultimately disapproves: such an approach would prepare a ruler who either spent his time reading books, contemplating the verities or extending his own realm, making him into, respectively, a mere student, a hermit or a tyrant. There is little pause or transition in Pasquier's narrative as each participant, or more aptly, each "voice" puts forward an often discontinuous and opposite point of view. With no real introduction, but perhaps building on what had just been said about books and philosophizing, Pasquier's *Politique* shrewdly sets up the *Escolier* to speak his mind on the ideals of kingship, first, and the *Escolier* is conscious of both his youth and his lack of experience compared to the others of their group, both key concepts to which Pasquier will return, in the present work as well as in the *Pourparler d'Alexandre*. Despite a sense of inadequacy the *Escolier* accuses the *Politique* of oversimplification. The *Curial* also baits the *Escolier* with mock encouragement. We shall see that although the debate turns against the *Escolier*'s arguments, aspects of Pasquier's own thinking process are represented in the *Escolier*'s stated points, as in those of each of the other "voices." He is also enjoying the experience of trying his hand at a Platonic dialogue. He is a recognized poet who insists often in his works on the value of "*lettres*"; hence the *Escolier*'s appeal to the muses as he begins to make his case, prompted by the *Politique* and the *Curial*. Similar to the *Pléïade* poets, particularly Joachim Du Bellay,[14] Pasquier's *Escolier* takes up the "*défense*" of the Muses, and of "*lettres*." To underline the prestige of his topic from the beginning, he declares that "*lettres*" speak for themselves and need no defense. He enlists the testimony of great figures of Roman history: He notes that Augustus favored a "grande flotte de poëtes qui furent en vogue sous luy," and that "we" favored them as a group. Other emperors, Tyberius, Nero and Hadrian, were poets *in their own right* in Latin and in Greek. The mention of Nero in a positive light seems strange, since the *Escolier* wants to underline the virtues of a good ruler. Perhaps he mentions both Latin and Greek as a parallel with the contemporary progress of French as a vernacular in competition with Latin, which now had the status among French men of letters that Greek came to enjoy among patrician Romans.[15]

From a calling of Roman "witnesses," the *Escolier* makes a sudden shift to French medieval ones. Pasquier has a special fondness for "Thibaut, comte de Champagne, par antiquailles et ruines se descouvre l'honneur de l'ancienne Rome." The *Escolier* recognizes Thibaut IV, king of Navarre, as an early ruler who was also a poet. The mention of "antiquailles et ruines" allows Pasquier to engage the contemporary vogue for works about local "antiquitez," archaeology, and also national origins. The *Escolier* reiterates the need to keep careful records of the past: "a careless antiquity" has almost lost trace of other great noble poets: counts Berlanger of Provence and Raymond of Toulouse, he declares. The *Escolier*'s stock of literary *exempla* stretches from the medieval period closer to his own time as he cites "our king of happy memory, François, and Marguerite, queen of Navarre." Similarly to Guillaume Budé,[16] in François' own time, he praises the royal siblings' patronage of "gens sçavans" and their own talents in verse: ". . . il semblait que toutes les graces de nostre poësie feussent assemblées en eux." (It seemed as though all the graces of our poetry had been assembled in them.) Having said this, the *Escolier* suddenly returns to antiquity with the image of Alexander's own largesse extended to Xenocrates, the man of letters, once again in a manner reminiscent of Budé in his *De l'Institution du prince*.[17] The *Escolier* catalogues other ancient men of letters who had been patronized by royalty: Pindar, at the time of the sack of Thebes; Virgil *tout court;* Sophocles for the strength of his tragedies; and finally Thucidides was restored to favor for his account of the Peloponnesian War, written during his exile. In brief, the *Escolier* concludes, the wisdom gained from books is useful to everyone. Books are a sure means of attaining to the good judgment and morals that accompany Plato's *sumum bonum*. A king prolongs the life of his realm by consulting sciences and "bonnes lettres." He gains peace of mind and can foresee the tide of events. He more easily keeps the peace with his neighbors and he enjoys prestige in posterity.

The *Escolier* invites the *Courtizan* (*Curial*)[18] to speak next, and he affirms the *Escolier*'s remarks. Such studies make sense in continuity with the preparation received in the colleges, and are sensibly linked to the *trivium* that prepares for philosophical studies. At this point the *Courtizan* finds it *a propos* for the *Philosophe* to speak. With complacency, the *Philosophe* asserts that his own views are contrary and superior to those held in the entourage of princes.[19] In this instance Pasquier's own thought is recognized by the reader. Kings (*princes* is the word consistently used in the *Pourparler* texts) are always surrounded by ambitious flatterers. The "voice" of the *Philosophe* serves to warn against them in this instance. The *Philosophe*'s discourse which follows is an analysis and ultimate refutation of the traditional claims of Stoics to represent the good life.

The *Philosophe* warns that the pursuit of luxuries and power leads most people to vices such as detraction and calumny (gossip) and they in turn become victims of these vices exercised by others at their expense. They are the objects of bad opinion and they give bad example. They are led by covetousness, the *Philosophe* insists. (This passage might suggest an image from Pasquier's reading of the *Roman de la Rose*, in the allegorical representation of "Convoitise" that the lover finds drawn on the exterior of the orchard wall.)[20] The *Philosophe* affirms that "convoitise" is like a ravenous beast ("bête allouvie") that torments the greedy with the passion for more gain, and the fear of losing what he has acquired. *Princes* should philosophize in order to keep their passions in check, since these are the enemies of reason. Pasquier uses brackets which Sayhi-Périgot notes disappear in subsequent editions of the *Pourparler*. In the brackets Pasquier or his editor writes: "The opinions of the Stoics." For the *Philosophe*, those deemed to be among the great (les grands) are really the least, while those who endure servile working conditions can be free in spirit. Pasquier pauses to criticize one of the popes, Boniface VIII, as particularly unfree in spirit. If the pope is traditionally styled as the "servant of the

Servants of God," Pasquier diverts the title, calling Boniface "the slave of the slaves." This pontiff was poorly judged in his time, by whatever prejudice, as an illustration of the unfreedom or moral servitude that comes with an inordinate love of wealth and influence.[21] (We note that in Book IV of the *Recherches de la France*, chapter 5 and following, Pasquier digresses lengthily over the various forms of serfdom that developed in French society which constituted a *survivance* from ancient Roman usage, and which continued. He is not critical of serfdom's continued existence, and he notes, without moral commentary, that historically, a serf could buy his freedom.[22]) Following the anecdote about Boniface VIII, a more directly dialogic form is adopted as the *Philosophe* interpolates the prince. How can one be a prince he asks, if he demonstrates no self-control or if he despoils neighboring states or his own subjects? The prince who argues for his noble blood falls back on a reputation gained by his ancestors, and he demonstrates no merit of his own.[23] (Pasquier believes in the French social order as such, and he is not an egalitarian. He mistrusts the popular classes. But he does state that true nobility lies not in outward trappings or in ancestry but in a life lived with virtue and a magnanimous spirit—perhaps here we can also recognize an echo of Rabelais for whom "l'habit ne fait pas le moine" (the frock does not make the monk), or of Erasmus's instructions for Charles V that a prince is not an ordinary person and cannot live a life based on comfort or on self-gain). What good is it for a prince to have the show of a bountiful table, with numerous servants at the ready if his mind is not well trained in the necessary? the *Philosophe* asks. He amplifies his critique in a rhetorical question: "Oh blind man!" he indicts him, "does the prince think that the accolades and applause are sincerely in his favor, and in the interests of his realm?" The prince must not be too ready to believe those who say the flattering or the reassuring thing. Pasquier brings historical images to bear on this question in the fortunes of Ephestion, and also of Alexander. Flatterers abound in a prince's prosperity but at the least sign of misfortune he finds himself abandoned and alone. The *Philosophe* gives vignettes about the similar misfortunes of other once-great princes, Darius and Nero, the latter of whom "heaped misfortune upon himself." He could scarcely find a single servant to help. As we have seen previously, Pasquier uses historical parallels to advise a prince—in this instance through the "voice" of the *Philosophe*—that stretch from classical to French national ones. "From the memory of our own ancestors," he warns, there was Charles de Charroulois, mighty in France and in Italy but who was undone by the Swiss. He was destitute of support, and died a "notorious" death at the "Journée de Nanssy" (Nancy)

(7 January, 1477). This was actually king Charles le Téméraire (Charles the Bold, or the Rash)1467–1477.[24] Following upon the tragic example of this king, the *Philosophe* emphasizes other Stoical *topoi*: a king needs to cultivate inner virtue as a mainstay for the realm against adversity. Agesilaus, for example, chose a lifestyle of personal austerity so that in adversity he would have no drastic changes to make. Alexander himself admired Diogenes' detachment of spirit, the *Philosophe* explains. Then, indicating the *Escolier*, the *Philosophe* conjectures that perhaps most will not rise to his exhortations, and he introduces the familiar theme of the world as a gigantic theater, also a giant scaffold holding the diverse figures of kings and commoners, that is, the run of humanity. In a borrowing from Erasmus' *In Praise of Folly*,[25] and perhaps also influenced by Pasquier's enjoyment of reading Rabelais, the *Philosophe* suggests that his own role is not unlike that of a king's fool, at whose antics it is permitted to laugh. He must be balanced in this role to interpret well human faults and impertinences. The mockery should be aimed at first towards self and should invite others to self-reflection. The *Philosophe* can be the butt of laughter, serving others as a mirror of what to avoid, when princes and their entourage are tempted to believe in material or worldly ideas. The carnavalesque is suggested as the *Philosophe* proposes that kings might exchange costumes with valets at the whim of a stage manager, perhaps in an allegory of *fortune*. The *Philosophe* suggests here the wisdom gained from various modes of experience. Pasquier enjoys an image of livestock attendants, shepherds, keepers of bulls or asses raised up to be kings (he seems to make no use of the biblical image of King David, as God's elect, chosen and anointed by the prophet Samuel from among shepherds, or for that matter, the image of the Nativity of Christ). Self-reflection and meditation on the tides of fortune, then, help the prince to avoid wars of ambition that derail stability and peace of mind and can bring death, decline and ruin.[26] In an ambient *topos* of the time, but which may also indicate Pasquier's familiarity with Montaigne's *Essais*, the *Philosophe* concludes that, since many kings suffered diverse arrears of fortune, no one ought to be regarded as having been happy until after death.[27] Our long reputation for greatness or virtue can be undone in a moment, the *Philosophe* insists, giving other names of rulers that kings, like all of humankind are made of the same clay, and they ought to have foresight against adversity and learn self-mastery.

The *Politique* is unimpressed with the *Philosophe's* harangue and he defers to the *Curial* (*Courtizan*) who brashly dismisses the *Philosophe's* arguments. (The *Courtizan* is another "voice" and a personification of the ambiguities that Pasquier finds most troubling in contemporary political and ethical arenas.) He complacently hands down that the *Escolier* is more to be pitied than mocked and although he would like to dismiss him from their discussion, courtesy forbids! We are nonetheless to understand that he confronts the *Escolier*, directly, with his contradicting stance. He complains that the *Escolier* had mere words and not solid arguments in his claim that kings ought to depend on books, and he tells him bluntly that he would have done better to keep silent. He declares that nations have risen by arms but have fallen by letters, thus he allies himself with much of the French nobility's traditional disdain for the latter. Through citing many instances from history to make his point he rather curiously notes that Adam, the first man, was illiterate and none the worse for it. He is certain that the princes cultivate letters only to impress, and that books are also for managing children. He calls the *Escolier* a "poor idiot." He refers to the origins of the world as a kind of *locus amoenus*, blessed by the absence of literary activities. Literary fronts are also used by rulers, he affirms, to impress the ignorant people who practically "demand" to be fooled by "telles piperies et fards" (trickery and appearances). He notes that Denis was skilled at manipulating the popular classes. (We note that Pasquier's use of a vocabulary of deceit lets him indict the "curial" class which he wishes to discredit as dishonest and disloyal to their oath to the king, which we recall that he mentions at the opening of the *Pourparler du prince*.) He is at war here against an ambient Machiavellianism which has crept into court circles thanks to self-seeking and manipulative Italian influences, which he will further discredit in the *Pourparler d'Alexandre*, and in many of his other writings.

The *Courtizan* now turns to the *Philosophe* and accuses him of pedantry. While a ruler ought to foresee, as best he can, the possible shifts of fortune, to worry unduly about the future is worse than what could actually come to pass. It is necessary to work in the present, he asserts, and the nobility is needed not for reflection and philosophizing but for action in defense of the ruler's interests. Now the ruler's interest is in promoting himself and in retaining power, nothing more, and his subjects exist for his sake. In the edition of the text of the *Pourparlers* to which we refer, either Pasquier or his editor has placed in brackets the indication [division générale du discours du Curial] (general division of the *Curial's* (*Courtizan's*) discourse). The *Courtizan* pursues his own argument: the king's greatness is seen either in feats of arms or in his laws. The latter are useful for the ruler to control the population. The following section of the *Courtizan's* discourse features a mixture of Machiavellianism and traditional commonplaces about how to approach matters of law. Both of these ethical positions would agree that to change laws would be to risk provoking popular dissent. While both traditional and Machiavellian discourse would recognize the need for strong military forces in such a case, the *Courtizan*'s tone takes on the cynicism that typifies the Machiavellian spirit: the ruler who wishes to change laws for his own personal benefit will simply crush popular unrest. (While this scenario is precisely that which occurred at the genesis of the *troubles*, Pasquier always advises *against* changing laws, to preserve the majesty of both king and Parliament and to avoid popular rebellion. His text also shows a *humane* concern, at times, to consider the "pauvre peuple," and, in legal proceedings, to avoid the exploitation of "les petits" by "les grands.") The *Courtizan* posits the contrary position: law and its representatives, the magistrates, are pillars protecting the ruler against "the ignorant people." Thus he creates a polarization between ruler and ruled which Pasquier warns can never last, and which in classical political ethics had been smoothed out by mollifying rhetorical political commonplaces and which actually did give a firm place to a pastoral care of the subjects, freemen and the indentured alike, by their rulers. The prince was typically advised to avoid meting out punishments that could be seen as too harsh, and also he should make a show of his *mansuétude* or forbearance. (Pasquier notes in Book I of the *Recherches de la France* that the king rules over a *free* people, as the term *francoys* means a free man.)[28] In Book IV of the same work he dwells lengthily on systems and degrees of freedoms that had been accrued to the French citizenry since late Roman times, in conjunction with law promulgated by good kings.[29]

The *Courtizan* suggests ways that the ruler can manipulate the people into giving money without resorting to force ("epuisent l'argent de leur people"). They can make claims of matters of great public ugency; they can also enforce stiff penalties on small "violations" that had not even been regarded as such previously. The *Courtizan* illustrates with examples, notably one about Denis of Syracuse,[30] whose false piety Pasquier mocks. Denis announced that jewelry was an inadmissible sign of vanity, and women, starting with Denis' own consort as a compelling example, were forced to surrender their rings, bracelets and the like under threat of heavy penalties. The profit from the jewelry was to go to build a temple to Ceres. Once the people's anger had abated and rudimentary temple foundations had been laid, Denis used the money for his own private purposes. He then renewed women's permission to wear jewelry ("a desire for which they are insatiable," Pasquier explains) on condition that they paid a financial offering to Ceres. The *Courtizan* explains that thus Denis succeeded in getting his way twice at the people's expense.

In regard to military matters, the ruler is well advised to conduct foreign wars as a means better to avoid civil ones. Such wars will not exhaust, but eventually replenish the ruler's treasury, the *Courtizan* asserts. The *Politique* then takes up his own arguments, and he specifies for the *Escolier*'s sake that many kinds of writers, including the Scholastics, are not necessary for the prince's education. He notes than an overly bookish prince is of no great value to the state, and that emperors Tiberius, Nero and Verus were Hellenised to no great advantage. He emphasizes that book culture did not prevent Nero's becoming a monster. Moreover, Pertinax, a simple carpenter, became a truly beloved emperor. Trajan, who was great, could scarcely sign his name. In brief, princes do not need the sort of education described by the *Escolier* for their successful performance in power. The *Politique* concurs that learning is in itself a "chose indifférente," and rulers are received well with, or without, a preparation in study; indeed, some of the more educated ones have met tragic ends. The nation then, continues, regardless of the prince's learning. There is a greater wisdom, of which Sparta, Rome and Venice offer fine examples: if the population can be prevailed upon to obey the magistrates and these later elaborate and apply the law, then there is a chance to breed into the people a spirit of self-sacrifice and willingness to die if necessary for the country. The *Politique* notes that in Rome philosophers were banned for a time, since they instilled in the young a sense of wondering and inquiry which diverted them from a spirit of patriotic service. (Here Pasquier uses one of his favorite turns of phrase: the young were taught (wrongly) to "bien dire" (examine ideas, articulate well) rather than to "bien faire" (respond promptly to then current calls for collective service and sacrifice.)[31]

Pasquier jumps from Roman examples to that of France's Louis XI, who did not want to allow the dauphin, the future Charles VIII, a lot of time in reading and in the disciplines. The *Politique* declares (and we can see this as Pasquier's own point of view) that he does not want to be that austere. The *Politique* cites Ptolemy's assertion (possibly from Pasquier's reading of Guillaume Budé's *Institution du prince*)[32] that it is useful for a prince to read in a book what his advisors are afraid to tell him. So, discretion in the *choice* of the prince's reading is important. After further determining what sort of literature is fit for the formation of a prince—some poets, such as Ovid, Catullus and Petrarch are dismissed as "poëtes folastres qui ne traitent que de vanitez, harengues, amusoirs d'esprit, tels inutiles exercices . . ." (vain, useless exercises)—the *Politique* asserts that the prince should indeed "philosophize" but seriously. The *Politique* recommends reading but especially: Plato's *Republic*, Cicero's *De Officiis*, and Horace.

The prince should read primarily about statecraft, as Scipion proposed to Cyrus. The prince needs to know Civil Law, but the *Politique* poses the question, as to whether Roman law is actually necessary. He notes the long history of effective jurisprudence in France, even when administered by unlettered officials, who had no background in Roman law and made no use of it. The *Politique* brings up the question of written historiography. Writing down a history is "chatouilleuse," he explains.[33] Historians can feel impelled to flatter the prince who employs them. The writer can feel pressures and fears and thus he can paint motives and outcomes in black or white as he finds it prudent. Pasquier's *Politique* gives the example of Philippe de Commines. Events and pressures caused him to flatter unduly Louis XI, while sometimes he reproaches him. Claude Seyssel reviles him in his history of Louis XII. The *Politique* calls Commines "a good valet" but is puzzled by what he sees as "je ne sçay quoi de mauvais traictement de ce roy" (a strangely critical treatment of this king), who first appears as petty, but then magnanimous and courageous. He compares Charles VIII and Alexander. The latter had no more reason to cross the sea with a few men to conquer Persia than Charles did to cross the mountains to possess Naples and Sicily. He compares the cost of such campaigns to their lack of results. After these remarks the *Politique* returns to his discussion of historiographers in the instance of Paulo Giovio, who has traditionally been seen as a flatterer for pay. Pasquier accuses him of lies and of covering up or denying French victories.[34] Yet he also credits him with showing French authors how to write narrative about their own kings.[35]

Continuing his discussion of historiography, the *Politique* affirms that historians can become too enamored of their own strategy to the point of being willing to falsify evidence.[36] Very interestingly, at the same time that he wants to have a true and accurate account of events, he also exhorts that the narrative be one that edifies, containing accounts of good moral and ethical conduct. The historiographer should strive to avoid the unfortunate model too often provided by certain preachers, who though well intentioned, are imprudent in their vivid descriptions of the vices of tyrants with the provocative, immoral details. Both the preacher and the historiographer have the responsibility to invite their readers/listeners to good conduct rather than plant potentially dangerous or morally blameworthy ideas in their minds. History is not merely a school activity, an indifferent classroom recitation about the actions of lords; rather it is an important and formative account of conduct worth emulating. The description of vices should not be belabored but stated simply as a warning about what to avoid. The *Politique* remarks that so rarely does one come upon such a fine example—there are so few guides, he laments, since "good" French historiography has been lacking. (This of course is one of the chief reasons Pasquier sets out on his own ambitious career as a writer, to provide a more popular, reliable and permanent account in the vernacular, of the historic, cultural and ethical values of French society. He also remarks that it is difficult to be dispassionate when writing about religion, and that one is most often "chatouillé de son particulier instinct.") It is challenging to avoid flattery of others or of one's own point of view. Human nature is such that the writer will drive home his case, whether right or wrong, Pasquier declares, through the "voice" of his *Politique*. The Horacian maxim that literature should both entertain and instruct is considered. He notes that in the case of a history, instruction is more important than entertainment, which is more valued by the common people: ". . . la plus part de ce populaire est coustumier de faire." He asserts that the *Annales de France* are informative but are not noted for an esthetically pleasing style. Paulo Emilio, moreover, was useful in instructing French historians in recording the facts of kings' reigns with greater precision. As Pasquier has jumped from one point to another in a rather disjunct manner, he now continues in this fashion as his *Politique* considers the *Chronique du seigneur de Langey*, which he cites for its lack of graceful style, but which, as it offers good *exempla* of desirable conduct, satisfies the reader, he declares, in its narrative about a lord who was known for military prowess, polished speech and facility in writing. With no transition, the *Politique* then reiterates his disagreement with both the *Escolier* and the *Curial* (*Courtizan*), at a juncture which helps Pasquier's hopefully patient modern reader to keep the thread of his supposed dialogue discourse, which in fact appears more like a series of juxtaposed monologues—*monographs*, really, that are rather transparently and flatly arranged, as we have said, to satisfy Pasquier's desire to articulate the various fragments of his own thought on contemporary issues, and which he supports with (an often tedious, though historically interesting) plethora of both classical and French historical and literary parallels. And so the *Politique* confronts the *Escolier* and the *Curial* (*Courtizan*) with what he determines to be their lack of argumentative substance. He repeats his warning about the need for discernment in the choice of the prince's reading matter. Not all books are of equal value, he warns. Some books, he explains, are like a landscape that seems from a distance to feature substantial intriguing detail but as we approach we see that it does not. (Metaphorically speaking, we have thus wasted a journey.)

The *Politique* then refutes the *Philosophe*. He sees his point, he tells him (Pasquier does not elaborate *how* he sees it.) but he is not entirely agreed.

Echoing Plato's *Republic*, in the dialogue about the just versus the unjust man, the *Politique* points out that the *unjust*, not only the just, can make use of virtues and vices to construct his own (skewed) version of contentment. Then, answering an earlier argument by the *Courtizan*, he declares that Denis was a tyrant to his people. He gives brief remarks differentiating kings and tyrants. A good king who reflects on the issues of importance is necessary for the people's well being, he affirms. He asserts that the *Curial* (*Courtizan*), however, has presented the image of a tyrant rather than a king. Directly addressing the *Curial*, the *Politique* confronts the former's rationalizations. The changes in law that the *Curial's* king would propose would bring ruin on the State. All laws, even bad ones, are better than ones enacted by caprice. Kings or magistrates who think that they are above the law cause scandal. In enacting laws, not just individual fiat but public procedure is important. In any good state, the people are answerable to the magistrates and these are answerable to the law. (It is noteworthy that the tone and style of argument here are very similar to Aristotle's *Ars Rhetorica*.[37]) In ancient Egypt, kings defended the law. The *Politique* paints the image of the ideal, iconographic French king seated on his throne, defending due process (before parliament) in a *lict de justice*, holding both the scepter and the traditional *main de justice*.

Continuing to rail against the *Curial* (*Courtizan*), he refutes the latter's Machiavellian tenet that the king rules only for his own gain. Rather, and as Pasquier notes in his *Recherches de la France*,[38] the king lives and functions in public, and he rules for the public good. The king who waives "*la primitive justice*" for what he perceives (wrongly) to be his present advantage dishonors himself and destabilizes the welfare of his realm. He who resorts to violence, in addition, usually has a short reign. In brief, violence, treachery and deceit are all to be avoided, declares the *Politique* in his refutation of the *Curial's* Machiavellianism. The prince's whole enterprise is to be always a *zélateur du bien public*. The *Politique* then deploys the *topos* of the *res publica* as a body, all of whose parts play their own essential role for the welfare of the whole. He gives the contemporary medical metaphor of the body, plagued in part by corrupt "humours" which over time, despoil the whole organism. Pasquier's *Politique* "voice" then jumps to an adage, perhaps reminiscent of his reading of Guillaume Budé, that the king, while he must be strong and self-confident, must avoid *hubris*. He must not have too lofty an opinion of himself,[39] because it is then that he is the least inspiring. The *Politique* gives vignettes about populations who, tired of their own grasping and tyrannical ruler, actually facilitated his downfall at the hands of foreign invaders. This they thought would at least be better for them than what they had been suffering. In this way Egypt, for example, welcomed Alexander, undermining their Persian overlords.

The *Politique* repeats here the *topos* that the king must have standing troops ready to defend the state. He notes that he agrees with the *Philosophe* that the king should agree to live relatively simply, not spending lavishly on his own household and so lightening the people's financial burden. In this same spirit, the king should avoid unnecessary foreign wars, since "burdens follow wars like a shadow follows the body." He recalls that in former times, kings were careful to wage wars at the least possible cost (no increase of *tailles* or *aydes* taxes).[40] Charles V and Charles VI both dealt with popular unrest over the issue of expensive wars, while the *Politique* praises Louis XII for engaging in *just* wars only.

The *Politique* raises the question of the just war. Through the "voice" of the *Politique* Pasquier insists that the strength and personal prestige of the reigning king and the choice of counselors mean everything in determining war and peace. He cites, as he often will in his *Recherches* and elsewhere, the instabilities experienced under Charles VI. Interestingly, Pasquier does not elaborate on the encroachment of the English during this reign, that, for example, Charles VI essentially lost power because of his mental instability and was forced to give his daughter in marriage to England's Henry V, who then claimed French legitimacy until the successful rout of the English forces under Charles VII: perhaps his national pride does not allow him to record English victories, although, by contrast in Book I of his *Recherches* he taxes Roman historians Caesar and Livy for failing to credit *Gaulish* prowess. Pasquier's *Politique* notes that stability was enjoyed under "good king" Louis XII. He notes that Claude Seyssel, too, praises Louis XII for entering into only *just* wars.[41]

Marriages and alliances, too, can be the cause of either greatness or ruin of a realm, the *Politique* affirms. The dialogic form is reinforced more overtly here as Pasquier's *Politique* addresses the *Curial* directly: "this is to show you, oh Curial. . . ." Charles V and Charles VI had built up arms to protect the people but at no small risk. Marriages, on the other hand, brought peace. Again, perhaps for strategic reasons of propaganda, there is no mention *per se* of Henry V of England. Pasquier gives simply a summary citation of examples where he believes marriages helped keep peace: with Brittany, Burgundy and Scotland. He then gives a series of examples of political marriages gone wrong.

Finance, too, can play a role in keeping the peace, as he shows in the example of the Venetian Republic, which almost never had to resort to military engagement. The *Politique* uses the Venetian example as a practical illustration of the *topos* that one must always avoid being at one's neighbor's mercy. Wars of expansion, as well, weaken a nation's focus and resources. Pasquier uses the metaphor of the walls of a weakened house that are only poorly shored up by dubious "helps" from without—that is, from neighboring states. He returns to his *leitmotif* that the best "walls" securing the realm *are found in just laws*, wisely thought out, tested by time and equitably applied. Without the rule of law all goes to ruin, the *Politique* asserts, and he cites another *topos*, that of Lycurgus, the giver of solid laws that helped Sparta to flourish. He then exhorts his audience to a personal, familial love of the good prince. Good subjects, he often implies, will naturally give their lives if need be, in answer to the prince's summons to protect the State; the prince in turn always feels the needs of the least of his subjects, and the reader/listener can suppose that Pasquier implies that the king will avoid needless military entanglements for their sake. The *Politique* further criticizes the *Curial's* (*Courtizan's*) view that rulers may force their will as they wish. He gives a transparent parallel with current French problems as he notes that certain Roman emperors indeed forced their will, aided by flattering legists. He asserts that a law is deserving of the name only if it is honored and not debased. It bears repetition that this particular point—the *sacrosanct value of the law* is a *leitmotiv* of most of Pasquier's writings, in the *pourparlers*, as we shall continue to see, as well as in the *Recherches de la France* and in other occasional writings including his poetry. Pasquier here borrows the metaphor of the *lion* for the French king, one which both England and Spain, France's enemies, feature also, in their royal coats of arms. (the French *fleur de lys* by contrast, stands not for the animal brute strength of the lion that here the *Politique* condemns in royal rule, but for reason and the theological virtues (the latter of which French kings sometimes took an oath to uphold, at the time of the *sacre*, or coronation). Moreover "our" kings are not like the Roman emperors in their lust for power but are "debonnaire." The *Politique* continues to draw a dichotomy with the vices of Rome: the Gauls, from earliest times enjoyed government under their own kings, who checked their own passions and submitted themselves to the law, which was administered by the courts. The *Politique* notes that historically the courts would give the kings *remonstrances*, reminding them that their conduct had to be in accord with reason. Pasquier's *Politique* gives what he calls an aphorism, a "memorable strategy of the court that ought not to be forgotten:" (". . . stratagème memorable d'une cour, et qui ne merite estre ensevely dans les tenebres d'oubliance". Pasquier narrates that Louis XI, whose character he describes as "remuant" (moody), threatened the court with death when it would not acquiesce to his whims.

La Vacquerie, the "most virtuous" first president of the court, with all other counselors appeared before the stunned Louis in their scarlet parliamentarian's robes. La Vacquerie told the king they would face death rather than ratify his edict against their conscience. Parliament won out and the king sent them away safely. Pasquier then reinforces a favorite principle of his: that the king is best served by a court that insistently reflects back to him the wisdom and truth of a proposed line of royal conduct. The king emerges the stronger and more loved by his subjects in his respect for law as administered by Parliament. In addition, in any republic (*res publica*) the Parliament serves as a useful buffer between the king and the people. This again will be another *leitmotiv* of Pasquier's political writings which he will illustrate repeatedly in various historical parallels. As the *Pourparler* draws near to its close, the *Politique*, who will have the last word, discusses the eventuality of a king's unjust use of public funds. He notes once again the unprofitable struggles represented by the involvements of kings in the Italian wars (in this instance, François I). In a final refutation of the *Curial's* thesis, the *Politique* affirms that a king best maintains his command of power by showing due respect for the laws and customs of his realms that he has inherited and whose best safeguard he must be. He gives the Ciceronian analogy of the good doctor (Parliament) that keeps the state healthy; as well as that of the notes of a musical composition that go together to create its beauty and harmony.[42]

In the *Pourparler du prince* the dialogic "voices" of the *Curial*, the *Escolier*, the *Courtizan* all serve a role in Pasquier's *disputatio*. Traditional Platonic and other *topoi* of just how much a prince needs to read and reflect, what sort of advisors he should engage and similar familiar themes are found here, and are supported or refuted in favor of rule by a good prince who himself submits to the established laws of the realm, as mediated by Parliament. Pasquier, who in his writings always represents parliamentary interests is heard in part in each of the dialogic voices but chiefly in that of the *Politique*. His *Politique* sentiments originated in his time in the *discours* of Michel de l'Hospital,[43] who warned of the need for toleration of religious, and other forms of *altérité* not as a virtue in itself but as applied practically for the welfare and integral survival of the State. Pasquier, like l'Hospital, was not uniformly moderate or tolerant in practice, as may be seen in the *invective* he deploys in particular in his largely constructed case against the Jesuits who sought the right to maintain their educational establishments in Paris. The anomaly of his reaction to the Jesuits aside, Pasquier who sought through his career and his writings to preserve French society in a time of crisis, always insisted on the centrality of traditional *law*, which is also his focus in a second *disputatio*, the *Pourparler de la loy*.

2. Le *Pourparler de la Loy*

A second dialogic text, which, like the *Pourparler du prince* just considered, can also be viewed as ancillary to the themes developed in the *Recherches de la France*, the *Pourparler de la loy* was published in 1581 by Gilles Robinot and reappeared subsequently with other publishers in 1596 and in 1607.[44] This work reflects tensions that by the late 1570s had reached an acute stage. A narrator voice opens the text with reference to the quality "chatouilleux de donner loy et permission a chacun de disputer de la loy général" (dangerous to give permission for just anyone to debate openly the value of existing law). French voices were raised in reaction to an aggressive dominance of much of political and cultural expression by ambitious and ethically objectionable Italians. The text opens with a brief reference to the troubling presence of *libertin*, a veiled reference to Italian) thought in the conduct of both personal and public life. The good suffer with the bad when corrupt officials interpret the law to their own self-advantage in this "malheureux siècle" (unhappy century) a locution that can recall Montaigne's reference to "ce siècle débordé" (this age of excess, this overwhelmed age) and which shows the pessimism or dismay[45] that in part colored the contemporary outlook regarding the possibility for a well-ordered society (and hence the need for Parliamentarians like Pasquier to write, in an effort to reinforce virtues and values. Thus we see a repetition and a bit more of a development of the theme of the fundamental and permanent respect with which Pasquier enjoins his reader to approach law, as it was treated in the *Pourparler du prince*.

The *Pourparler de la loy* follows the dialogic *topos* of a conversation between galley overseer and slave, but here there are two slaves, thus three participants who argue theses and counter theses that Pasquier has already outlined in the *Pourparler du prince*, and which he deepens here. The text furthers the ambient discussion, in the Early Modern period, of the continuing presence and role of a variety of forms of servitude. This is not surprising in a society still characterized by signs of feudalism.[46] The most celebrated discussion of the topic of servitude was La Boétie's well-known *Discours de la servitude volontaire* (1548), to which Sayhi-Périgot refers also.[47]

After the narrator's introduction, the first two participants are introduced: the *comite*, a sub-officer of the galleys, and the first galley slave, while the third character, the second galley slave, will intervene much later.

The first slave calls on the *comite* for decency and recognition of his quality. (This in spite of the crime which as the reader will learn, has caused him to be condemned to be a slave in the galleys as his punishment.) The *comite* is doubtful: "Who is this who regards himself as being of value? His *interrogatio* allows the first slave to set up the dichotomy between the appellations "barbare"—an identity he denies for himself but assesses as appropriate for the "inferior" French. And he cites his own (superior) birth in "flourishing" Italy and "worthy" Rome. Having established his superior national origins, he styles the eternal city as "ruler of the Universe" and "home of the Holy fathers." Thus the text acknowledges the dual menace for Pasquier of ancient Roman prestige (as it overshadows French cultural identity) and the "Holy fathers," the Roman Church's imperative to direct internal French ecclesiastical affairs, a concept repugnant to Pasquier and his fellow Gallican parliamentarians, albeit they remain confessional Roman Catholics. The first slave also identifies as a philosopher. The *comite*, an allegorical voice of France, interpelates him as "philosophe-pendart" (philosopher-rogue) and with a collective "nous," charges the the slave (an allegory for all Italians) with "delicts." He declares that the slave is "Italian, Roman, yes, but no philosopher." The *comite* then identifies himself as a man of influence who has been separated from studies too early in life. There ensues an epistemological argument as to how does one learn best, by study or experience. He also invokes the role of virtue and man's post-lapsarian condition. The *comite* appeals to the Aristotelian *topos* of virtue as its own reward, that the slave's current unhappiness is a consequence of vice. The first slave then cites the condition of good but fallen man and that, alas, a momentary failure in judgment only has been consequential for him as well as for his fellow slaves in the penal colony. The *comite* then invites him to tell his story, since there is time. Here as somewhat further on in the *Pourparler de la loy*, Pasquier's narratology becomes more clearly literary. The slave embarks on a casuistic discourse opposing perceptions of law as opposed to the demands of necessity. The slave suggests that acts which the *comite's* conventional values call crimes: murder, theft, *paillardise*, may often be committed under the duress of circumstance and thus culpability may be mitigated. The slave favors his own subjectivity as opposed to existing law. The *comite* then offers a traditional counter argument, denying the credibility of the slave's position. Unchecked passions including the profligate use of money have lead to ruin for many in their time, he asserts. Thus Pasquier sets up a fictional parallel to counter the moral and legal imbalances he perceives in his own day. The first slave counters the *comite's* arguments and asserts that philosophers of the Aristotelian and Stoic schools are hypocrites, and that generalizations are ill advised. He gives two examples of philosophers whose bogus casuistry allowed for sensual license: in a particularly misogynistic image, Aristyppus, like the sun, descended to "gutters" but was not soiled by them. Diogenes, too, gave himself license in sensual matters. Pasquier characterizes Diogenes as a "folâstre" poet. This is an adjective he employs in the context of his early love sonnets, a term which denotes whimsy, *folie*, and also the pardonable and endearing weaknesses of youth. The slave then, asserts that all philosophers are hypocrites, disguising and renaming in virtuous terms their various passions as they have wit to do so, and they fool only the simple-minded with their "beau parler" (casuistic *persuasio*). In her notes to her critical edition of the *Pourparlers* Sayhi-Périgot records that the Stoics, particularly, were commonly cited, in the Early Modern period, as the type of the hypocritical philosopher. It is also well known that Montaigne and Pasquier were intrigued by, but then rejected the Stoic school. The slave too, in a different manner than the parliamentarians, has rejected the Stoics and acts rather as a *desboché* (debauché). He decides never to suffer but to enjoy the pleasures of life as they come to him, which has as one consequence that he finds himself condemned to the galleys.

The thesis of Pasquier's dialogue between the *comite* and the slave at this juncture would seem to be that philosophical schools and study are useful as long as they instruct in the practical truth about human nature. Both participants in the dialogue, of course, have contrasting views of what that nature is, and what sort of discipline will help it flourish in useful ways. The slave declares that he has reevaluated received ideas and that nature is henceforth his base. He is ironic as he poses the rhetorical question as to whether legists and physicians claim that their laws derive from nature. He has reconsidered everything, he declares, and he exclaims that the laws against larceny are tyrannical. This is perhaps an example of Pasquier's taste for Rabelaisian methodology in his narrative—the ironic, the carnavalesque and the world-upside-down, which offer means of counter-argument and its *amplificatio*. The slave continues in this vein as he notes that for him, revenge was outlawed by cowards. A note of phallic humor intervenes at this point in the narrative. "Copulation" (practices) is moderated by men of "little effect"—not much sexual prowess?—who "mesurent le commun devoir. . . ." (who regulate the propriety of frequency of marital function according to their own (meager?) capacities). The slave continues to jump from one theme to another. In our original, natural state, he continues, all men shared alike in the common abundance without hierarchical or economic distinctions. An economic discourse continues as he notes that with the coming of the concept of private property God himself seems to have been recast by some men as an "idol of stone, no eyes to see my merits, no ears to hear my prayers—heaven sends me (the slave), a disaster, a wretched life." Thanks to the (perverse concept) of property and its safe-guarding, he asks what (was available for him) to steal? The real culprits, the wealthy, (who hoard what naturally belongs to all) go unpunished, while they steal more than he does, and it is simply called by a different name. He declares that common people are cheated out of a just price by inflationary practices. The *comite* intervenes to cite the seventh commandment of the Decalogue, "Thou shalt not Steal." The slave retorts impatiently, with his own definition of theft and those who are more guilty of it than others. He opposes his own case, that of the simple *larron*, who steals by necessity, with the "true thieves" as he styles them who first established boundaries, walls, regulations, and laws, with the concept of inheritances and possessions. It is significant to remember that Pasquier's first slave, who styles himself as the "larron-gendarme," a sort of "social conscience" by self-definition, is *Italian*. He personifies the ambient French perception that the Italians wish to dismantle existing French law to install their own self-interested version of it. The "world upside down" figure represented in the slave's utopian discourse is reminiscent of that of Erasmus, More, and Rabelais.[48]

The *comite* suddenly cites the Universities, like that of Paris, as guardians of values, only to be refuted by the slave: he joins the ambient criticism of University teaching in the period. They award uninspired masters in arts degrees he complains, with which students leave able to cite verses from *Florilegia* but without developing habits of deeper thinking about values. We noted that Pasquier's own ideas are often reflected even in the voice of his antagonists in these dialogues, and the slave's criticism of University pedagogy would seem to be another reflexion of Pasquier's reading of Rabelais. In a rare textual structuring, the *comite* and the first slave exchange a number of brief interactions between the long speeches that are normally featured. The *comite* replies to the slave's assessment of "revenge": which he characterizes as the "mother of murder and misfortune." The slave counters that revenge is a normal reaction to those who wrong us. Pasquier sets up this opposition between the two participants to underline his own support for existing law and Scripture, particularly the Decalogue, from Exodus and Deuteronomy as well as from Pauline exhortations. The open conflict between traditional classical and Christian ethics and the "Italian" (Machiavellian) casuistry represented here by the first slave is seen in these exchanges. The *comite* cites the Gospel mandate to love evil doers, not their evil actions, and the slave counters that this particular exhortation is more "advice" than a true commandment.

"We Italians," he points out, value the refusal of forgiveness, especially in the case of insult. Here the text illustrates a practice Pasquier often uses in his writing, of inserting material in one work that he has used in others, in this instance, a discussion of dueling as satisfaction for insult, which he also discusses in his *Recherches*.[49] The *comite* dismisses the first slave's arguments as "merveilles" (fantasies, strange ideas). The *comite* declares that the first slave's values are conflicted and his attitude towards women, in particular, is scandalous.[50] Perhaps Pasquier moves on an impulse to impress the reader with his medical knowledge, and we wonder if he had experimented in dissecting cadavers.[51] As the first slave discourses further on sex, and particularly about the sperm ducts (vaisseaux spermatiques), he reasons that it ought to be as permissible to speak about such bodily functions as one would about the flow of blood through the veins. The *comite's* retort here is key to Pasquier's thesis about the Italians—he tells him that his discourse has some merit but that it is skewed. Had he been wise, the *comite* conjectures, the first slave could have lived successfully by the laws of his country. As a persuasive strategy, the first slave returns to a softer, more personal tone that he featured at the opening of the *Pourparler* as he appeals to the *comite's* "humanity." He is but a victim of "fate" and dire circumstances which forced him to act unlawfully. The slave's entreaty may reflect the scriptural desire of the sinner not to be treated as his sins deserve but to win compassion, again, through his *persuasio*, since he is really good by nature. The slave never admits to actual crimes but exonerates himself and calls on the *comite* to do so as well.

The third participant of this *disputatio* is suddenly introduced. There are certain metatextual elements first: In brackets (in the 1582 edition) Pasquier notes that "the Frenchman enjoys free speech." The critical editor of the *Pourparlers*, Béatrice Sayhi-Périgot, notes that this section, in italics, disappears in the edition of 1596 and after. Does Pasquier change his point of view? It is also of import to recognize that the text is based not in historical or antiquarian perspectives as is true of some of Pasquier's *corpus*, but the issues here concern chiefly ethics and moral philosophy. The text then signals the (arrival) of "le vrai philosophe" (the true philosopher). The second slave will give a counter point to the "Italian" arguments of the first slave. In what is predominantly a politico-legal discussion, the second slave briefly alludes to anthropological and ontological questions, just as the first slave had addressed the *comite* about medical and biological ones. The second slave declares that philosophers such as the first slave wear such "masks" that he can hardly tell the qualities of a "true" philosopher. The "masks" are chosen by men to dissimulate their "animalistic" appetites. He implies by this statement that it is therefore with difficulty that one can decide what is real and constant about human nature and values. The sex drive and the more fundamental instincts (self-preservation and ambition) would seem to be a common denominator. The second slave announces that he for his part is a "native of the world."[52] This is a common expression of the period, used by Pasquier himself in a letter, and of course it suggests nascent anthropological attitudes based in works by André Thevet[53] and others, and on which Montaigne (sometimes using Thevet's text) would base some of his own observations on the relativity of law and culture according to places and peoples. At the second slave's declaration that he is a citizen of the world, the *comite* remarks that this is nothing new, signaling perhaps that this is an ancient Greek boast once again circulating in French thought. The second slave continues in a vein of anthropological relativism: while the Italian boasts that he is from Rome, and no barbarian, he insists that even barbarians have their own good reasoning according to the diversity of places—good sense differing by region, where each happens to live, a conjecture with which the *comite* agrees. The second slave gives a critique of the first slave's theses: he, the first slave, is a "typical Italian braggart." we know that Rome conquered but then was subdued. Rome remains only in name.[54] Its law was eroded to become license, and today there is no freedom in Italy. With an air of superiority, the second slave notes that in Italy, morality is practiced haphazardly, and so this slave (the first slave) is in the predicament where he finds him. Thus the third participant of the *disputatio*, the second slave, claims superiority over the first, even though the outward context of their criminality and prosecution has dictated their mutual condemnation to the galleys. It would seem that these galleys are a metaphor, a stage for the discernment of what is real and lasting in the human spirit and its values. Can values be discerned and can people experience a *metanoia* in their reasoning, even after apparent definitive failure? Is failure really definitive or can science and argumentation help to raise the spirit and the sense of belonging to one's own society, its norms and established laws, even in apparent personal and religio-political chaos? These are questions that would seem to be imposed by this text. The second slave goes on to refute the first slave's tenets; private property is not theft of what originally belonged to all. He is wary of the first slave on these matters as well as on his arguments about common sense, law and the tenets of the Christian religion. The *comite* ought not to be taken in by him, the second slave warns. The above is a jurist's commentary in dialogue form, about how to shape human behavior and values.

A dialogue ensues between the first and the second slave, with brief intermittent remarks by the *comite*. The first slave ponders the ramifications for the power to choose right from wrong, if the second slave's assertions were to be true. The second slave explains that reconciling philosophical and ethical differences is to be desired, but let this be done in less consequential venues. He returns to the thesis, expounded at the beginning of the *disputatio*, that too much open debate weakens the authority of the law. He analyzes the *humors* that dictate personality and color one's reasoning, and which result in the diversity of opinions. He gives a vivid tableau of the flights of dream imagery that can accompany the sensations of those governed by each of the humors. While one's humor dictates opinion and reasoning, free will is still in place and allows to follow the objective laws of the land, necessary precisely to insure order amid the diversity of humors and their colorations of potential individual impulse. One's attitude as to what is bitter or sweet should be conformed to the "tastes" of one's countrymen. The intellect, too, can be seen to err if it does not conform to the *mores* common to one's own country. The passions themselves can best be kept in check to allow for true freedom to follow the law rather than to be a slave of impulse. Trouble comes since the individual is deeply grounded in his own first impressions which can militate against open-mindedness, dialogue, and obedience to what lies outside the self. It is interesting here that Pasquier says nothing about the effects of the fall of Man as disposing him to concupiscence. Copernicus and Paracelsus are invoked in turn. The former stood out by shattering the theories of his forerunners, having defended the thesis that the earth moves but that the heavens do not; Paracelsus dismantled the old theories of medicine.[55] He declares that the new doctrines of these scientists came from the powers of their intellect, at which point the first slave warns against making too sure a generalization of much detail without discussion. Even beasts know enough not to return to a place where they have been beaten, the second slave rejoins. The first slave enquires whether the ancient principle of cause and effect has any foundation. It can be remembered here that the text then is representative of the genre of the *disputatio*, which airs disparate views even if one particular argument is supposed to emerge as the correct one.[56] Pasquier continues to display both a scientific and a philosophical bent as the second slave poses the question as to whether sensate knowledge is the only reliable way of knowing the external world. The earlier editions of the text then feature brackets around the statement: "This would seem to take us far from acknowledging the Providence of God." He further remarks that some use the senses as their means of knowing the Universe. There follows a further discussion of the diversity of opinions: the pre-Socratic philosophers receive consideration, notably Thales and his theory of heat as the foundation of all life. The discussion sums up some of the leading points of the science of the period, while the discussion closes with the supposition that life is regulated by a "maistre-ouvrier" (master laborer). Editor Sayhi-Périgot sees this inclusion as a "prudent" means of closure of the discussion, a concession on Pasquier's part, perhaps to avoid ecclesiastic censorship. Does she view Pasquier as a shrewd positivist posing as a theist merely for prudence's sake since he has mentioned the views of Copernicus and Paracelsus? This appears to me to be an either-or stance that has in an unnecessary way characterized much contemporary criticism of sixteenth-century authors.[57] In the current critical view, an interest that an Early Modern humanist might show in science, especially Copernicus, "demonstrates" his or her rejection of Christian religious belief as a remnant of the irrelevant past. The critic has thus made a deliberate and fragmented choice of focus, as M. de Certeau explains.[58] Pasquier then mentions academic skeptics who suppose that the soul is reducible to the brain, the heart or the blood, and he disagrees with that analysis. Pasquier's rule of thumb, as explained through the voice of the second slave is that principles held by the collective common sense are a guide to find certainty. Thus he rejoins and answers the initial thesis that too much debate about established laws (and other national mores) is ill advised and that conformity to the laws of one's country on these matters leads to the happy life under the rule of a "good" king, that is, one who takes advice from parliamentarians, like Pasquier. The second slave elaborates these key points with a reference to Lycurgus, known as the personification of the giver of permanently valid law, together with such terms as "infallible" and "irrevocable," all supportive of Pasquier's thesis that the law must indeed be permanent and unquestioned. He also returns to the hypothetical scene of the advocate of a new law who appears to the people with a cord around his neck. If the popular response is unfavorable, the one proposing it is to suffer "une mort honteuse" (a shameful death). To avoid unwise changes in law, Pasquier 's second slave emphasizes, there is a need for the public to trust magistrates, those who know the law better than themselves. Interestingly, the *comite* intervenes to quote the *Koran* on the inviolability of the principle of law. In a series of seemingly disjunct interventions, which, again we recall are characteristic of the genre of the *diputatio*, the second slave suddenly points out the possibility of exceptions to any law. The *comite* then exhorts that there is a great difference between law and *faith*. The second slave emphasizes that *idiots* should not dispute *the* faith.

At this juncture it should be pointed out that for parliamentarians, law and faith were of a piece in the Early Modern period, in prudent government, and that bishops as well as secular lords held seats in the Parliament and were counted with them among the peers of the realm. The second slave then expounds upon another key point, the twin of the axiom about the indisputable character of law—that an identical attitude should be adopted in matters of faith. The "diversité des opinions" opens to the possibility of heresy and its attendant factionalism "rendering government difficult for the magistrate." As a means of continuing the argument, the first slave wonders why the second, clearly a religious man, has been condemned to the galleys. The *comite* echos the question which invites the second slave's solilioquy on the fate of the unwary just person, exposed to a world of self-interest. His good nature, not a crime, brought him to this end, he explains, to which the *comite* rejoins "merveilles!" (How strange—wishful thinking).

The second slave narrates the events of his personal undoing. The text here includes some of Pasquier's key ideas that can be found scattered throughout his various other writings; they also include an effort at a more entertaining and more literary style, which rejoins a *leitmotif* of the "world upside down." He "sought to avoid" the "chicanery" of the "great court of lords." Pasquier, though he extols the judiciary and its virtues, also warns against the corruption that l'Hospital and others denounced in court procedures in the 1560s. The second slave describes his one-time happy life as a utopia: He "thought of the needy" and was "generous with money" and with "advice," for which the people held him to be a "king." He deems that he "*was* a king," figuratively speaking, and there follow *topoi* descriptive of virtuous kingship—he exercised "good judgment devoid of passions;" he was, in Pasquier's stock terms, a "zélateur du bien public," crying out against injustice, and against the "abuse of the small by the great"—themes to which Pasquier often returns in his writings. "All was for the best," the second slave pursues, as though from some "original chaos" there had sprung "order." He warns against looking too much for ultimate answers in life's mystery, that answers are in the "hands of God," not in those of "unjust, petty tyrants." He declares that the too aggressive pursuit of honors and too much self-concern are vain. Thus he supports indirectly the Aristotelian principle that the good life lies in balance, the exercise of virtue and the avoidance of vanity. Yet the jealousy of "fortune" deprived him of his happy estate. The second slave's "goodness" is accentuated in the rejoinder of the *comite*: he is "too good a soul for the galleys." The second slave declares that officials arrested him as a pretext to confiscate his considerable wealth. The *comite*, defensive, rejoins that judges couldn't possibly be so lax. The second slave then seeks to persuade that "judges are guided by witnesses and procedure only." The second slave takes on the allure of a *Job* figure in that he long-sufferingly understands all as perhaps permitted by God, for some greater good. The *comite* marvels at his patience even as he has been condemned to the galleys. There is a repudiation of stoicism in the second slave's brief reply, that his patience is not "one made of stone" but rather learned by long experience. He recognizes the common misery of humanity in the ambient "great chain of being" motif, and the galley becomes a metaphor for the human condition: he recognizes that not only he himself, but princes, kings and magistrates are all in a way poor, rowing in their own "galleys." The great become slaves of their own desire for more status. Ambition is itself a slavery of agitation and worry, he concludes. A documentation of the dilatory effects of inappropriate ambition is another leitmotif for Pasquier's writing in his efforts to preserve traditional French values. The *disputatio* ends as the *comite*, who represents legitimate law, recognizes the second slave's philosophical wisdom and conjectures that he, the second slave ought to rule, and they exchange a pledge of friendship. The motif of the world upside down recurs as the second slave affirms that while he himself suffers physical discomfort, he enjoys peace of mind, while for the great and powerful, the opposite is true.

3. Le *Pourparler d'Alexandre*

The third and last of the *disputationes* that accompanied later editions of the *Recherches de la France*, the *Pourparler d'Alexandre* was published for the first time in 1581, at the same time as the *Pourparler de la loy*. Pasquier continues the characteristics of the *disputatio* genre which allows for a range of ideas to be suggested. Rabelais, perhaps Pasquier's favorite author, and who came to personify a Socratic, "gadfly" presence in literature, is his vehicle to further explore the complexity of political personalities and motivations. The *Pourparler d'Alexandre* then, opens with the character of Alexander the Great, who is perplexed that members of his own family have allowed personal greed and ambition to dismember his great empire. This narrative serves Pasquier as a parallel with his own preoccupations with the inherent threats imposed on French internal, and external security by the death of a strong king, Henri II, and the dangers during a successor's minority that power can fall to vain and ambitious princes of an inferior sort. Pasquier addresses the problems of regency periods in *Recherches* II, 19 as well as in a another section of the same work, even more pertinent, on the dismemberment of Charlemagne's empire, after his death, by his own sons. Pasquier does not wish this history to be repeated in the instance of the weak successors of Henri II, and he supports the regency of Catherine de Medicis, who he admires, against the ambitions of princes of the blood.

A *leitmotif* that recurs in this text from the two previous *Pourparlers* is the observation that respect for both human and divine law is increasingly lacking. The historical-literary parallel with Alexander, for whom the text is named, and the portioning of his empire allow Pasquier to see the same threat of *division* present in his own time and to make it the topic of this third *disputatio*. Another literary borrowing, namely, the character Rabelais serves Alexander (and Pasquier) to reflect on the shifts and turns of human nature, of history and of the ethico-political landscape. Both Alexander and Rabelais seem to be voices of Pasquier's reflection, and especially Alexander represents many of the ethical and political *topoi* that he has already mentioned in the other *Pourparlers* and in the *Recherches* as well as his other occasional writings and in his correspondence.

Alexander and Rabelais review the history of the treachery that has been visited on the princes of Alexander's own blood, at which Rabelais retorts that he had warned him of as much, and that he, Rabelais, had not been the first to do so. Alexander insists that he always ruled with benevolence and that he built a fine government, which others have now despoiled. In a strategy that may recall Rabelaisian *amplificatio*, he gives a list of the conquered cities. Rabelais notes that Alexander's captains all vied for the crown, and that the ablest got the *febve*, a term Pasquier seems to favor, as though to imply that a crown fought over for motives of vain ambition is reducible to a parlor game traditional for *la Fête des Rois* (Feast of the Three Kings,)[59] in which contestants draw for the piece of cake containing the "*febve*" (bean), which makes them king or queen of the feast. Pasquier uses the term "febve" to draw a key parallel between the wake of Alexander's reign and the troubles of his own time, in which many have come to approach government, power and the crown itself as a mere game of chance where the persistent and unscrupulous player will win the prize. The Rabelais voice notes that "blood," in changing politics is more effective than "ink"—again a comparison Pasquier teases out also in the *Recherches de la France*, regarding "chevaliers" who "spill their blood" in the king's service, and the "noblesse de robe," a new kind of "chevalier," offering worthy service, Pasquier insists, but who "spill" only "ink." The "blood and ink" comparison employed by the Rabelais voice suggests that violence has held sway over reason and advice, the printed word or the dialogue of diplomacy. Indeed, the Rabelais voice continues a tone of parody and irony as he explains to Alexander that, since his death, a new sort of government has taken over among *les grands*: *ambition*, a shrewdness and a quality he calls *chiche*, or *avariciousness*, suggesting that a lack of true availability to *le bien commun*, has now crept in. The Rabelais voice as well as Alexander's continues an ironic or parodic function throughout the text: he suggests to Alexander that only people with generous hearts want to rule, and that at times, Alexander's equals in courage have not enjoyed the same good fortune he himself has. In a key phrase, Rabelais tells him that such persons *take* their opportunities, *even against the law*, and then find justifications. They look for pleasures and possessions. Alexander never had to resort to this, and his experience had combined prowess and good fortune. After Rabelais' observation he explains that if he was so successful it was because he was of good character as opposed to other conquerors who live in fear of an uprising lead by those they have displaced. When Rabelais reminds him that there is method in destroying utterly the conquered rulers, Alexander remembers that it is innate in people to prefer to live under the authority of their own native prince. Here again and throughout the text, Alexander's narrative will provide a historical-ethical parallel with the French national experience of Charlemagne's sons and the threat of violence or displacement of legitimate rule at times of war or dynastic transition.[60] That the people desire to be ruled by their own native prince is a parliamentarian construction: as Sayhi-Périgot observes in her notes to the *Pourparler du prince*,[61] the participants of that dialogue simply contrive to assume that the best form of government is kingship and that "the people" naturally prefer this form over any other. Pasquier always makes this self-serving declaration, throughout his writings, and exhorts the sentiment that loyalty to the king (and thus to Parliament) is synonymous with being "un bon français" (a good Frenchman). Rule by one's native prince is for him and his fellow parliamentarians, the only regime that is, to cite M. de Certeau, "pensable" (thinkable, imaginable).[62] The text demonstrates Pasquier's frequent habit of citing classical, French historical, and scriptural (or more generally Christian) ideas in the same exposition. The Rabelais voice speculates about the relative place of fortune and calculation in the fate of rulers: having just supposed that the people prefer their own native princes and will be loyal to them against a foreigner, he then conjectures that they may just as easily prefer whatever ruler gives them better treatment, and that finally, the fortune of kings is unpredictable.

He gives the examples of Augustus and Julius Caesar: the former slaughtered his opposition but was beloved by the population; the latter was benevolent but finally assassinated by those he had helped. The Rabelais voice supposes, in a biblical vein, which could also be seen as classical in origin, that no one can escape his fate. Some may rationalize the outcome of events, but God alone disposes and God's ways are not ours. We have only the present, to be used well. We must endeavor to use good judgment towards whatever is in our power. This *exhortatio* may be directed towards the Valois rulers and their lieutenants. The Alexander voice continues in this vein and repeats some of Pasquier's most privileged *topoi* of good statecraft. Alexander warns against alienating any part of the royal domain. He notes that he gave parts of his domain to his captains to gain their loyalty. Perhaps this is a parallel with the selling of titles and other forms of venality that Pasquier complained about under Henri III. Alexander also warns against the curse of a bad conscience. He insists that his own is at peace since his actions were always "royal." He explains that, although he took the crown at a tender age, he put the affairs of State in order. Perhaps here Pasquier makes an unfavorable comparison with the weak rule of the young and sickly Valois princes: François II, dominated by the Guises, which fact provoked the Amboise Conspiracy, the Civil Wars of Religion, most particularly, under Charles IX, the Ste. Barthelémy; as well as the further extremism of both the *Ligue* and the Huguenots; and the chaos during the reign of Henri III, who ordered the murder of the Guises. Alexander tells Rabelais that he notes that (the French) "vous" are free ("francs et libres"). The Rabelais voice interestingly, makes no response, and this assertion seems to be an isolated one as the Alexander voice jumps to a different theme. He emphasizes that his acts were not ones by which he ever sullied himself or had a need to feel remorse. In another key exchange for Pasquier's agenda in writing, the Rabelais voice invites Alexander to affirm that his government exercised authority in keeping with Natural Law,[63] to which the emperor affirms that it did, and that thereby he also secured his own happiness.

Rabelais further asserts, that as now, dead, "we" would be presumptuous to be concerned with what is thought by posterity. The deceased ought to contemplate much loftier things, although Pasquier does not have his Rabelais "voice" enumerate what these are. The deceased should avoid occupying themselves with law, or with "vile, earthly things in which one muddies one's thoughts." This remark of the Rabelais voice is particularly ironic given the predilection, in the *Pantagruel* and the *Gargantua*, for commentary that touches on law and custom, which he often colors with the "muddy," the earthy and the scatological. Alexander chides Rabelais for his reference to these "low" concerns and fears that he may begin to doubt his own accomplishments in government, and the quality of his reputation in posterity, which he insists he always sought to guard unsullied. Rabelais reassures him that he is regarded by mortals as the paragon of kings; that he undertook all of his acts with bravery and success, prudently and without temerity; to which Alexander declares that those who claimed he lacked prudence were guilty of the same fault. He affirms that he was well born and had only high and magnanimous desires, while Providence too, gave him Fortune as his escort. Rabelais continues to assuage him, praising his "chastity," his diligence and ruggedness, "as he himself had declared," he tells him; Alexander believes his "sincerity" and basks in the praise. This exchange gives an indirect reference to the *topos* that kings should avoid flattery and not be too avid for even sincere praise, which is dubious at best in the present instance.

A more comic turn in the exchange is seen as Rabelais quickly brings the emperor down to earth, speculating that some in posterity may suppose that his vices outweighed his virtues. A balance is hard to achieve, he muses. The unwary Alexander is stunned and surprised. Rabelais now hammers him. He notes that in warfare, Alexander was more the conquered than the conqueror. He loved conquest and valued more his ascendancy over the revered Greeks than over the Persians. Alexander interjects only brief comments, perhaps to underline his shallowness, or his wounded vanity.

Rabelais confronts Alexander with the *hubris* he demonstrated in deifying himself and his relations, who were *francs et libres*, not barbarians, from other nations. This is a key point for Pasquier, as both the citizen and the prince should favor their own society and never alienate any part of it to a foreign power or seem to be inferior, or vulnerable to external political pressure. Pasquier mixes more of his enjoyment of Rabelais in the next exchange, a bacchanalian one, in which Rabelais, himself a trickster, accuses Alexander of the same and sees also as an unpardonable fault his failure to provide enough wine for guests! Moreover Alexander failed to pardon his close friend Cletus, who was, in addition, his maternal uncle and his mother's brother. Whimsy plays a hand as the text places these two faults on an equal moral footing.

All of the foregoing exchange between the two participants deals with a *leitmotif* of Pasquier's agenda in writing, which he raises from the outset of his career, in the introduction to his *Recherches de la France*, and in his chapters in that same work on the Gauls: kings should be careful in their choice of advisors and in what and who they believe. To insure a good record as well as a useful guide for posterity, they should be transparent and virtuous in a life of balanced and thoughtful stewardship of the realm, which will be recorded by careful and honest historiographers, not flatterers or tricksters, roles that both participants in this *disputatio* play in turn. Rabelais who used parody and irony in his own works, appears in this text under similar modes, to advance Pasquier's critique of contemporary conditions and behavior and to suggest reform, in some cases, or a return to traditional French values, in others.

· 4 ·
LAW AND THE CHRISTIAN TRADITION IN FRANCE

"O que bel est le proverbe françois par lequel nous sommes enseignez qu'il faut laisser le moustier ou il est, voulant dire qu'il faut rien aisément remuer de l'ancienneté!"—Pasquier, *Recherches* III, 7.

1. Gallicanism and French Relations with the Popes

It will be helpful to discuss Pasquier's attitudes towards the Church and religious observance as these were central preoccupations for him, as for the sixteenth century. And of course Pasquier wrote in the context of the nine successive Civil Wars of Religion. The citation above recalls that as a Parliamentarian he presents to his reader an acceptable or "receivable"[1] magistrates' interpretation of law and traditional French values that he wants to see predominate in matters of national religion (le moustier l'Eglise) as well as in all other aspects of French legal, political and social life. In Book III, he does not simply present a history of the Catholic Christian experience in France, but he uses examples from ecclesiastical history both in France and in Italy to give polemical guidelines for French ecclesiastical affairs.

He is interested in demonstrating that in the past—*ancienneté*—there were examples of law and other precedents that can serve as safeguards against an uncertain future. In the years following the Council of Trent, which called for papal jurisdiction over Church affairs in each nation, too much change or influence from abroad was not useful to the *Parlement's* need to retain power, also in the wake of the feudalism and Roman heavy-handedness of previous centuries and the continuing uncertainties of present times. Pasquier explains to Pithou the contents of Book III: "Celuy qui explique la discipline ecclesiastique de France et les privileges de nostre Eglise Gallicane auquel je pense avoir expliqué tout ce qu'il y a de bon et de beau à ce sujet."[2] Thus he presents book III as a *compendium* of the French ecclesiastical experience. Gallicanism as Pasquier articulates it in Book III stems from the Pragmatic Sanction (*la Pragmatique)* of Bourges of 1438, in which kings began to assert control of the national Church. Pasquier borrows the term "gallican" from Yves de Chartres, an author to whom he returns often, and uses it to denote a national Church for France, one which maintains its union with Rome but in which the French hierarchy, nominated by the king, is solely mandated to oversee Church discipline within the realm. For Gallicanism, the king, not the pope is the court of final appeal in all French ecclesiastical matters, to the exclusion of the pope and his *nuncio*. Recourse is occasionally had to the advice of national ecclesiastical councils for important matters, and which have ultimate say, again, under the king, independently of any reactions by the popes. Pasquier asserts that this arrangement has been understood historically by both France and the papacy, not without moments of disagreement or efforts at retraction, as popes were historically mistrustful of councils and sought to avoid them.

2. Heresies of the Past to Be Avoided in the Interests of National Unity

Pasquier for his part is proud that such a legal system has given greater unity and order to French church life. Moreover, he is pleased that the Church in Gaul had, historically, been free of "les damnables et mal-heureuses heresies de l'orient."[3] This notation regarding the past is significant of course given the current history of domestic religious wars. In an effort to instruct the present, he insists that "heresies" bring divisions, and he repeats this principle often in his rather complex personal policy enunciated in his *Recherches de la*

France and in his *Correspondence*, as well as in his occasional writings. Also in the *Correspondence*, he views "Genève" as the chief source of the religious conflicts. Pasquier saw the national Gallican (Roman) Catholic Church as an arm of the parliamentary monarchy and a cement of French society. As we can feel authorized to say about the majority of his contemporaries, Pasquier was a believer. Like most parliamentarians, he practiced the Catholic religion. He states this unambiguously in Book III of his *Recherches*. Even in the profession of his own religion he couches his affirmation of it in traditional and legal terms, which can arguably be said to be his most comfortable form of discourse in approaching any of his topics: "Nostre regle generale est, qu'en France nous devons vivre en la Religion Catholique, Apostolique Romaine . . ." (Our general rule is that in France, we are to live under the Roman Catholic, Apostolic Religion . . .).[4]

3. Pasquier's Personal Piety and Appeals to His Reader

Did he hear mass on a daily basis with his family or with his colleagues, as Montaigne can be supposed to have done in his private chapel in the library tower on his estate,[5] and if so, was it a matter of personal piety, a *pro-forma* observance, given his station in life, or a blend of both, as Montaigne for one, would seem to view as characteristic of *le branle*- the inconstancy of human living and motivation? At the end of his introduction to book III Pasquier speaks of his own sincerity in writing. He appeals to his reader to bring to his text "the same 'candeur, roideur et sincerité' that I do." Pasquier refers at various points of his text to his self-identity as a Catholic. He points to details mandated by that identity: For example, the baptism of his new-born son Theodore took place at the church of St. Nicolas du Chardonnet in Paris, 8 November, 1560[6]: this church was his own parish where he visited and conferred with parish priests and even with certain Jesuits with whom he was individually reconciled after the famous controversies; we hear from Montaigne that Pasquier took the last sacraments on his deathbed and that he was buried in the Church of Saint Sévérin, though, not altogether surprisingly, given the desecrations during the Revolution, there remains no trace of his monument there today. In her biography based on Pasquier's *Correspondence*, Dorothy Thickett notes that he wrote commentaries on the four Gospels, though none of these particular writings seems to have survived.[7]

4. Religion, Law and the Need for Continuity

In keeping with the central theme of the present book, Pasquier's efforts to preserve law and cultural values in his time, this chapter will focus on Book III of the *Recherches de la France* in which Pasquier articulates his appreciation of the French Christian tradition, where it has been, and what must be done to preserve "le moustier où il est," and to safeguard the functional aspects of the French church's "ancienneté." In Book II of his *Recherches*, Pasquier manipulates history to make polemical points about the central role of good ethics under a good king, always guided by the *Parlement*. Book III In turn is written in the context of the domestic confessional conflict while France was also under potential threat from Spain, Italian ambitions, proselytism from Geneva and from what Pasquier styles the potential for interference in French affairs by the popes and their legates in France.

5. Book III in Relation to the Other Books of the *Recherches de la France*

As is true of the other "books" of Pasquier's *Recherches de la France*, Book III has no special title of its own. It was published for the first time only in 1596 in Paris by Jamet Mettayer and Pierre l'Huillier, the latter of whom had published Pasquier's works before, and it was augmented in 1607 and in 1621. Pasquier had delayed publishing his works after some pilfering by other authors who had failed to credit him as their source. Books I and II appeared in seven editions (Book I alone in 1560 by Jean Longis; 1567 in Paris by Simon Calvarin; Book II in 1565 in Paris by Claude Senneton; 1567 in Orléans by Pierre Trepperel; and Books I and II in 1569, by Pierre l'Huillier in Paris; 1571, Claude Micard; 1572 the same; 1581 in Paris by Giles Ribinot and in 1594. Finally in 1596 Book III as well as the two previous and books IV, V and VI appeared. Books I through VII appeared in 1607, 1610, and 1611 and 1617; Books I through IX appeared posthumously in 1621 (Sonnius), 1633; (Olivier de Varennes), 1643 (Pierre Ménard), 1665 (at Orléans, Charles de Sercy), 1723, Trévoux, Amsterdam.[8]

6. Pasquier's Tone and Intentions in Book III

A word about the tone and intent of Book III that concerns religious affairs in France. I have just noted that Pasquier wanted the established norms of French law to govern, in the person of the king as informed by Parliament, the internal affairs of the French Gallican Church with its traditional privileges and exemptions that he will discuss. Parliamentary control of the national Church, including its regulation of religious practice would have been the norm given the fact that the peers of the realm, who sat in Parliament were composed of both secular and ecclesiastical lords, and there was as yet no separation of Church and State in the time of "Une loy, un roy, une foy." A recent rethinking of the degree to which Michel de l'Hospital was a tolerant figure, may also be in order in regard to Pasquier's own attitudes.[9] I shall demonstrate that Pasquier's tolerance was tempered by contemporary mentalities and by the strategies he saw as expedient to put forward to maintain the Parliament's ascendency in French religious affairs. He always manipulates anecdotes of history to a polemical and a political end. He promotes traditional values and bends the logic of the Christian (Catholic) religion to promote his *Gallican* parliamentarian agenda for control of religious affairs.

7. Continuity with the Ecclesiastical Past

As a lawyer who is interested in social and political systems and in the roots of law and procedure in *ancienneté*, Pasquier opens Book III with a thorough analysis of the earliest foundations of Christianity as instituted by Christ himself. He piously refers to *Le Seigneur* (Christ). He appeals to the scriptures, particularly to the narratives of the four Evangelists and to the extra-scriptural teaching of the Church known as *tradition*. His own narrative is perhaps reflective of his misgivings about the not too historically distant events of the Council of Trent, which, largely inspired and directed by Robert Bellarmin, codified Christian beliefs in the *Catechism of the Council of Trent*. The resolutions of that Council, advocating strong papal authority over national churches were not well received by the Paris Parliament. Book III of the *Recherches de la France* is largely Pasquier's own *plaidoyer* in which he instructs the reader in the historic relationship between the Church of Rome and the Catholic Church in France, which with his parliamentarian colleagues, he always refers to as "nostre Eglise Gallicane" (Our Gallican Church), and he describes the necessary autonomy of that Church, under the authority of its own bishops united with the king of France, and he relates how that autonomy was won, the debt in which the Church of Rome still finds itself in regard to France because of the latter's historic aid to various popes. Finally he relates historic vignettes to put the reader on guard against a well-documented tendency of some popes to interfere, despite agreements in national church affairs. Finally he also offers the caveat against "new sects and religions" that have sprung up and which pose a potential threat to national security and unity. Book III then, is an apology for the Gallican Church and an effort to protect its prerogatives in the context of the Civil Wars of Religion. Pasquier was not alone in writing in defense of historic Gallican privileges: his friends and parliamentarian colleagues, Pierre Pithou, Jean Du Tillet and Claude Fauchet, to name three, all wrote their own treatises on the Gallican Church for reasons similar to those that impel Pasquier.[10]

8. Book III and Gallicanism

In Book III, 34, Pasquier devotes a chapter to propose strategies by which the Gallican Church can protect its ancient freedoms from "abuses," as he calls them, proposed by the fathers of the Council of Trent. Pasquier lists what he calls the "four pillars" of Gallican Church freedoms: the "appel comme d'abus," (right to appeal); the "Holy Decrees"; the Royal Ordinances; and the Acts of Parliament which he asserts, since they are given by divine mandate itself, cannot be modified or cancelled by any authority of "la cour de Rome." By this reasoning a French king cannot be divested and the kingdom cannot be placed under papal interdict, open to being siezed in such a case by any foreign prince, or by Rome itself. Pasquier allows that the Council of Trent accomplished many good things, chiefly that its documents form a resumé of the principles enunciated in previous church councils. In wishing to shore up the Roman Church's authority against "ceux qui se sont séparés de nostre Religion," whose objective had been "le terrassement du Saint Siège de Rome," they wanted archbishops and bishops to derive their authority and policies of action from the pope, to show in what high respect the Petrine office was to be held by all. Of course Pasquier and his parliamentarian colleagues were very far from any such *ultramontain* assertions of *Trent*, but the times were given to a greater codification of beliefs, laws and procedures, and this informs his method that pervades his own *Recherches de la France*, no matter what the topic he has at hand. So Pasquier can be said to begin Book III with the tone of a modified *Trent*, or more precisely, a *Gallican* Catholic Catechism, at least in tone, if not in thoroughness of method and content, and in the context of the Civil Wars of Religion that are still not ended at this book's appearance, is designed to make clear what is to be held, and what is to be discarded, by *un bon français*, as he will also refer to himself, in some of his occasional, polemical verse. The discourse used in Book III is at times theological and catechetical. He describes the original unity of the apostolic church just after the time of Christ. He cites an anonymous work from the time of King Charles V ("le sage") for which he has high regard: *Le Songe du vergier.*[11] He notes that this work is "digne d'être enchassé dans ce livre." He cites one character, le *chevalier*, who voices the foundations and *raison d'être* of the Church: ". . . il faut considerer en nostre Seigneur deux temps, celuy d'humilité avant sa Mort et Passion, celuy de gloire lors qu'après sa Resurrection, il fut monté aux Cieux. (One ought to consider two moments in the life of Our Lord, that of his humility, in his Passion and Death, and that of his Resurrection and Ascension into heaven.) He cites the same text in reference to Christ's sharing his authority with Peter and his successors, the future bishops and especially the line of the popes: ". . . nous ne revoquions point en doute que Saint Pierre ne fust le Grand Vicaire de Nostre Seigneur Jesus Christ. Consequemment que tous ces mesmes privilèges avoient esté transmis en luy et ses successeurs." (We have no wish to suggest that there is any doubt that Saint Peter was the Vicar of Jesus Christ. Consequently all the same privileges were transferred to him and to his successors.)[12] Thus here Pasquier cites a theologically oriented text, *Le Songe du vergier*, and nothing authorizes us to suppose he did not believe the Christological doctrine that it enunciates. However he uses this text, and also direct citations from the four Evangelists to demonstrate, in keeping with his Gallican agenda, that Christ distinguished between his own, divine authority, and that of temporal society, the famous distinction about rendering to God what is God's, and to Caesar what is Caesar's. Thus he builds his case, supposedly based in the authority of Christ's own words, for the independence of the Gallican Church from any jurisdiction by the popes. He is here as always, primarily a lawyer. He asserts with the use of this same text the autonomy of French kings from the temporal authority of the popes. This casuistic form of argumentation characterizes Book III, where he also argues for the Church's original unity, making use of the principle of the deposit or faith, and the Apostles' Creed; as opposed to its present *disunion* due to what Pasquier believes to be a prime cause of political and social unrest, the *diversité des religions*. In regard to that diversity, we know that like many intellectuals of the sixteenth century on any side of the confessional debate, Pasquier held his own (Gallican Catholic) convictions but kept up a dialogue with others of diverse confessions in the spirit of the free exchange of ideas,[13] as much as this could be practiced. It is important to note that while Pasquier's *Correspondence* testifies to his close friendship with a number of reformers, he never publishes any religiously unorthodox opinions, apart from his Gallican interpretation of the Petrine office, and he rarely speaks directly of Catholic dogma, and then only affirmatively, in Book III and elsewhere. Pasquier uses historical citations to insist by implication that Providence always guided the Universal Catholic Church "as a monarchy like no other." Very significantly for Pasquier's preference for pacifism where possible, he affirms that the Church prevailed not primarily by force of arms but through persuasion. Pasquier does give a brief critique of papal military campaigns and situates the papacy and its growth in influence in the historic context of the Church in Italy.

The post-Apostolic, Patristic periods of Church history receive attention. Church fathers such as Irenaeus and Tertullian wrote to promote the unity of the faith and the integral character of Scripture, and they fought heretics such as the Marcionites and other Gnostics. Pasquier's focus on Irenaeus, who insisted on the unity of Scripture, may be a veiled parallel for his own insistence upon, at first, the unity of one religion in France, but later, on an allowed pluralism of confessions, with these placed clearly under the authority of the one king of France, directed of course, by Parliament. It has to be avowed that while Pasquier would ultimately see religious pluralism as the way out of the civil conflicts, he does want to maintain the religious *police*, or administration of France in contiguity with *ancienneté*.

Pasquier affirms in ch. 1 the divine origin of the authority of the popes as the successors of St. Peter, to whom Christ had given the mandate to lead the Church (Matthew 16:17–19) He notes that although there existed the worthy patriarchates of Alexandria, Antioch and Jerusalem, over time, Providence had elected Rome as the primary see to which all others looked as the seat of the universal church. He asserts in harmony with Christian tradition that Rome's ascendancy was a natural consequence of having been the place of the martyrdom of St. Peter, and that all popes from Peter to Sylvester had died as martyrs and had been *recommendable* in virtue and in the exercise of their duty. He notes that popes came to enjoy the status as "universal bishop," in large part due to the holiness of their example. Pasquier speaks about the duties and ambitions of popes in the same vein he does of the kings of France.

I have noted that Pasquier uses historical parallels to instruct in law, ethics and cultural values for the present. He asserts that a measure of *disunion* has always existed in the Church, and thus he seems to imply that such should not be surprising, though it be very regrettable, in his own time.

In the midst of describing broad principles of Church history into which he will assert Gallican rights, privileges and values, he pauses here as well as elsewhere, notably in Book VIII, for a close analysis of titles and their etymologies and their current meanings. Just as in Book II he analyzes the various classes of secular society and titles that accrue to them, so in a discussion of the succession of the popes he shows a lawyer's taste for discussions of procedure and precedence. He pauses over the popes' title "votre sainteté" and how it came into use. We know that Erasmus had paused over the use of this same title for Roman pontiffs, in his conduct book written for the young Emperor Charles V.[14] Erasmus approved of the title, as he thought it would keep the pope mindful of the virtues he needed for his office. Pasquier notes the New Testament reference to God as "abba," a familiar Aramaic name for "papa," indicating ease of communication between human beings and the divinity. He discusses the appellations of direct address for priests: "père," or father, which would indicate a prolongation of the tone of "abba" and a reminder of the obligations of a pastor. Also, the title "abbé" is mentioned. Very interestingly, these sallies into word descriptions also serve to remind us of the ethical duties incumbent upon those to whom these names and titles were addressed. The title for the Roman Pontiff, "Pape" simply meant "grandfather," Pasquier reminds. He notes very significantly that this later title of "pape" came into use in "L'Eglise prennant nouvelle discipline par nouvelle devotion." (The Church taking on new discipline to accommodate new forms of devotion—my translation).[15] Is his reference to "new discipline" for "new devotion" a simple assertion that the Church's practices and self-understanding changed principally by the external dictates of new times and circumstances, as George Huppert asserts;[16] or is it more specifically Pasquier's recognition of what the early Church had understood about its own process of doing theology as a reaction to the lived experience of the Christian faith? Or is it a veiled suggestion that changing times called for a new tolerance of alterité in forms of Christian expression—the Huguenot phenomenon, that Pasquier and his Catholic contemporaries did not understand or embrace but which they ultimately accepted for the peace of the realm? All these are hypotheses. There remains room for Pasquier's acknowledgement that the Church changed over time within his own conceptions of Gallican Catholic orthodoxy, however. But Pasquier's text that precedes and follows this rather isolated statement about "new discipline" and "new devotion" is in fact at least a tacit affirmation of the titles of the pope and their significance. He has just explained the title of "universal bishop" and moves onto a consideration of the pontiffs' efforts at an imitation of Christ-like humility in another appellation: *servus servorum Dei* (Servant of the servants of God). While Pasquier supposes that the effect on believers would be more similar to that of "king of kings," used by the Persians, inspiring awe and trepidation rather than a sense of the pope's servanthood, these texts in Book III authorize us to suppose that for Pasquier, the Petrine office had become and ought to remain one of universal reverence and spiritual jusrisdiction, except for as we shall see, in what he calls the *temporal* internal affairs of the French Church. I return us now briefly to the opening of Book III, where Pasquier has added a disclaimer: as he will assert the authority and right of French kings to govern the affairs of the French church against any interference by popes, still Pasquier finds it prudent to state: "si protesté-je ne le faire en intention de vilpender la grandeur de celuy que nous avons toujours reconnu et reconnaissons pour le chef de l'Eglise: ains parce que la necessité de l'histoire me le commande, et que ce sont mesmes fautes à celuy qui descript l'ancienneté de pallier un mensonge, comme de taire une vérité."[17] (I protest that I have no wish to slight the one on whom we all have looked and continue to look as the head of the Church; the needs of history may decide for me—and it is the same fault to gloss over a lie as it is to keep silent about the truth—my translation). Pasquier of course has his own views of the *needs of history*. He will discuss the human frailties of popes just as he does elsewhere those of French kings, since both have an obligation to give good ethical example and have often failed.

9. A Central Theme in Pasquier's Program: Attaining Good Counsel

Pasquier recommends good counselors to popes as he has to kings. Good counsel and law make a kingdom endure, and religion is one of the fundamental elements of society, he affirms. French kings Clovis, Charles Martel, Pepin and Charlemagne had all been of great help to popes, and Pasquier will insist, as one of the tenets of his Gallicanism, that the popes historically have owed a debt of gratitude to French kings. These kings therefore are entitled to be critical of the Holy See, and are exempt from excommunication by the individual decision of a pope, and their kingdom may not be alienated from them by an act of Rome.

Pasquier cites St. Hierosme to assert that Gaul had always been loyal to the Christian faith and that it had been free of heresies. This affirmation can be seen to rejoin Pasquier's other assertion, in Book I, that Gaul had always flourished under its own kings until the Roman occupation by Caesar. One can perhaps surmise a parallel in Pasquier's mind: if ancient Rome and its propaganda had caused the decline of the Gauls, Modern ecclesiastical Rome must not be allowed to eclipse French kings and the guiding hand of the Parliament. The religious unity that Pasquier asserts as having existed down through the line of Clovis he cites as a necessary historical parallel to instruct the present: while the people may forgive ecclesiastical corruption as it happens, an edifying example is necessary. When writing history he says, one must make full account of both vices and virtues. He gives a précis of Christology and ecclesiology, a brief dogmatic survey that he believes will be familiar to his reader: "Comme chacun sait." He appeals to common knowledge of the Christian cultural-religious memory.

Very interestingly, Pasquier included in his published correspondence a letter to Guillaume de Marillac on the topic of "Les ordonnances d'amour,"[18] afirming that the impulse to love in all of its forms, especially erotic and romantic love is a human value held the same from one time, culture and religious confession to another, a point reminiscent of Montaigne's observations about the relativity of cultural *mores* in *Les Coches*. Yet we see that Pasquier also affirms, in the *Pourparlers* the wisdom of adhering to the *mores*, including the religious ones, of one's own country, an axiom also found in the *Essais*. Thus Pasquier can assert his own cultural and religious Catholicity, as we have seen. Pasquier gives a long apology for the *spiritual* primacy of the popes. Long before the late nineteenth century definition of papal infallibility at Vatican Council I, that doctrine had been widely held in the church. Pasquier draws the necessary dichotomy between the human failings of men, given concupiscence, and curiously says nothing related to the doctrine of Original Sin as the prime source of human inclination to corruption. He affirms the doctrine that despite a pope's human potential towards corruption, papal authority *in matters of doctrine and morals* remains inviolate. He does not use the word "sin." Perhaps as a lawyer he prefers to make use of a legal and rhetorical lexicon rather than a theological one, where possible, and even his theological and ecclesiological discourse sounds more like that of a lawyer speaking on these topics. He draws historical parallels with contemporary ecclesiastical affairs. He criticizes corruption among ecclesiastics who all the more, for their reform, are and should be under the king's jurisdiction rather than that of Rome. Pasquier's critique of clerical *ambition* and his equally critical remarks about the cardinals of the Roman Church are reminiscent of satirical verse on the same themes in his fellow poet Du Bellay's *Les Regrets*. We recall that unlike some Protestant reformers, Pasquier never calls for a dismantling of these ecclesiastical institutions, but again, like Du Bellay and Ronsard, he does call for reform *from within*. To that extent we can identify him with the Catholic Reformation. He sees the Roman hierarchy as a seamless system of command based in the doctrinal principle of the apostolic succession. He accepts that current-day ecclesiastical authorities form a hierarchy the origin of whose authority is from Christ and Peter and their successors down through history. The clergy and the prelates, in order to be authoritative themselves, are necessarily in *union* with the pope, and the pope is the visible sign of union for the Universal Church, once again as stated by St. Irenaeus. Union then, is key in Catholic Christian doctrine. But Pasquier asserts that papal authority and the union spoken of in doctrine is by nature *spiritual*, and again with a lawyer's command of rhetoric he makes an artificial and fairly indefensible dichotomy from the point of view of Catholic-Christian doctrine, asserting the pope's *spiritual* supremacy in the universal church, while affirming the Gallican tenet that the successor of Peter does not have any jurisdiction whatsoever over the *temporal* affairs of the Church in France. Anyone familiar with the New Testament and with Christian doctrine particularly from Saint Paul will recognize that this position is contradictory to his claim to defend the faith and the primacy of the papacy. His argument is contrary to the Pauline discourse of spirit vs. flesh. Paul emphatically affirms that the flesh, or the the *temporal* as Pasquier refers to it, is only complete when governed by the *spiritual*. Pasquier's references to Scripture and Christian tradition in his rather contrived defense of Gallican privileges is to be expected by the modern reader, since for medieval mentalities carrying through the sixteenth century, scripture and tradition were regarded as forms of law. He therefore naturally makes reference to them while adjusting their meaning for his own polemical ends. Reading Pasquier's text, the reader is reminded over and over that he is a trial lawyer, as he brings out "evidence" that is, points of history or of contemporary occurrence to argue his "case." As he often makes use of polemic, so we will see that he also employs the ambient invective of his time at the expense of his opponent.[19]

Pasquier continues his discussion of the popes, and their growth in influence and security, which he attributes chiefly to the support of French kings from the time of Charles Martel, Pepin and Charlemagne. Pasquier explains that, more than other rulers, the kings of France historically supported the

See of Rome in its universal sovereignty. In that sense, French kings continue to enjoy the universal influence once exercised by the Gauls, Pasquier appears to imply: ". . . car elle fut bastie du commencement sur une pauvreté obstinée, sur une affliction continue, sur un martyr juré."[20] So Pasquier emphasizes that the popes needed and accepted help by French kings. In exchange, the French Gallican church had received certain *libertez*. He analyzes the development of these freedoms and privileges in the course of chapters about the first and second dynasties 'Lignées' de nos rois." (Dynasties of our kings). It was at this time that principles of Gallican ecclesiastical law were worked out: Pasquier reminds us about the details in different segments of different chapters of Book III: the pope may not alienate the French king from his kingdom; nor can the French king be excommunicated or otherwise condemned by the pope. These points are a response to historic episodes where popes attempted, through various "fulminations," to control the policies and internal affairs of certain kings. Pasquier describes the progress of papal authority in Rome and the growth of what would become the Papal States. In his discourse about the relationship of the popes and French kings, which extends through the first half of book III, he notes that Pepin, Charlemagne, and Louis Le Debonnaire did much to confirm the popes as well as their own status in regard to their mutual duties and prerogatives with the papacy. He accentuates the ambition and moral weakness of the historic personages he describes. For example when he speaks about the moral lassitude of some kings, he notes dryly: "il y eut de l'homme en nos rois." (Tell what it was—There was (too much) of the man (and not enough of the dutiful sovereign) in him.") We are always reminded that Pasquier's discourse about the past is also instruction and qualitative commentary about the present, with concern about the hopes he can have for France's future: "A quel propos tout cecy? Non autre, sinon pour monstrer comme les affaires de nostre Eglise Gallicane se trouvrent adoncques vagues et fluctuantes pour l'injure du temps et que pour vray dire, il n'y avait rien si certain que l'incertain." (What is the point of all this detail? None other than to describe how the affairs of our Gallican Church were then vague and drifting by having been neglected over time, and if truth be told, there was nothing more certain than uncertainty.)[21] Pasquier often returns both to a detailed description of Church discipline and procedure as well as to the controversial effects of clerical and pontifical *ambition*. He describes the manner in which the Roman pontiffs extended their influence over bishops both in France and abroad through the use of insignia of office, notably, the *pallium*.

10. The *Pallium*

A strip of white wool woven with black crosses and worn over the other vestments of a Christian prelate, the *pallium* is a symbol denoting primacy of jurisdiction over a diocese or an archdiocese and is featured in the earliest artistic iconography of bishops and certain saints in the Western Church. It signifies that its bearer is in union of obedience with the pope. It implies that the wearer will follow the same ecclesiastical and political policies as the pope and *la cour de Rome*.

Pasquier complains in ch. 12 about the venality of offering favors to other ecclesiastics responsible for one's own promotion. French bishops thus enjoyed papal preferments as Pasquier believes, "at the expense of our ancient freedoms (liberté). He cites the *pallium* as "l'un des plus grans instrumens qui se trouva lors, et depuis pour asservir nos prélats . . ." (. . . one of the most significant instruments then as now, for subverting the loyalty of our prelates). "Chacun se rendit par une ambition particulière esclave, afin d'estre come Vicegerans du S. Siège en France . . ." (Each one through personal ambition (thus) made himself a slave, to become so to speak, ancillaries of the Holy See in France . . . .) Pasquier recalls the particular historical vignette in which Foulques, the archbishop of Reims, complained to Pope Formose that the subjectively bestowed *pallium* was provoking confusion and disorder in the Gallican Church. Some of inferior rank in the hierarchy were receiving it while in some cases their Metropolitan superiors might not. Moreover Pasquier notes that Foulques believed the honor was debased when given indiscriminately even to some clearly unworthy (indignes). Here we see Pasquier speaking out against venality in the awarding (and selling? he is not specific here) of ecclesiastical honors, in this instance as a means of controlling the French Church, just as he has also spoken in Book II and in his correspondence, against the selling of honors by kings to raise money for their personal projects, including unnecessary wars. Pasquier notes that the *pallium* in his view was problematic and divisive for the Gallican Church historically and continued to be so in his own time. He also notes that more generally, recourse to papal approbation of the election of bishops could be used locally as a means of dishonest advancement, as in the case of the election of the five-year-old Hugues, the son of Bonon, bishop of Chaalons, as archbishop of Reims. The facts were carefully hidden from Rome and Abbon, bishop of Soissons, actually managed the archbishopric of Reims and its funds during Hugues' minority. Pasquier gives this illustration to point out that in his view, Rome could not possibly manage the internal affairs of the French Church with much clarity or accuracy and that local ambition had taken advantage of that well-known situation. All the more reason for the maintenance of Gallican freedoms with regard to the Roman primacy, which thus in theory avoids the possibility of mismanagement by both Rome and the French Church. We also observe here a special concern of Pasquier's that he has previously applied to *secular* politics, namely, the dangers of ambition that can easily attend a king's minority. He transfers the same caveats to the event of an elected prelate who is a minor. Once again he insists, French law and precedent are the best guarantees of peace and sound government in the ecclesiastical as well as in the secular arm of the French parliamentary monarchy.

Given the exhaustive use Pasquier makes of historical *exempla* to argue for the importance of preserving the Gallican Church and its freedoms, not to mention his tendency to repeat himself on these issues, it is perhaps best to limit our discussion to a few more excerpts of his texts that can be thought to be representative of his preoccupations with ecclesiastical affairs.

11. Jean Gerson and Institutional Memory

In Book III, 16, Pasquier argues that a "Concile general et universal" has supreme authority in the Church, even over that of the pope. In a manner reminiscent of the medieval scholastic appeal to "auctoritas" in arguing one's point, Pasquier invokes Jean Gerson: "Jamais la faculté de Theologie de Paris n'eut un plus grand Theologien que maistre Jean Gerson . . ." (Never had the School of theology of the University of Paris so great a theologian as Master Jean Gerson.) At a period when some literary and Evangelical figures whose works we know Pasquier admired, such as Rabelais and Marot, were critical of the Paris theology faculty or the Sorbonne, Pasquier places himself squarely in harmony with that institution and its rights to have a guiding—and for him—to be sure—a welcome hand in all ecclesiastical, intellectual and cultural matters. Again we see that Pasquier's attitude signifies that much of the medieval edifice blending law and religion had remained intact in the minds of parliamentarians and their contemporaries. Thus Pasquier regards Gerson, himself a many-sided and international clerical figure, as also a lawyer of sorts. He had been active during the Western Schism, which Pasquier discusses in ch. 25. For Pasquier, Gerson is a towering figure, one who combined in his own accomplishments membership in both the ecclesiastical and the secular governance of French society and who had helped to see France through times of religious conflict similar to the contemporary challenges. Like Pasquier Gerson was a poet and a champion of valuing the vernacular in many of his works. Gerson as chancellor headed the most important theological faculty for Pasquier's arguments in Book III of his *Recherches*, and as he asserts the authority of Gerson, who had been an accomplished orator like himself, he also implies that other, disagreeing voices are not welcome or to be seen as credible. He describes the essential contents for his reader of Gerson's work, *De auferibilitate Papae ab Ecclesia*. (On the Power of the Church to Depose the Pope). This particular choice of focus on Gerson's part is curious since he was named chancellor of the University of Paris with the approbation of the "antipope" Benedict XIII, "Pierre de la Lune" (Peter Luna), who Pasquier is at such pains to discredit in ch. 24. After a disclaimer insisting that neither Gerson's text, nor he himself calls for a suppression of the institution of the papacy in the Church, he stresses that the "greatest theologian of France," Gerson, saw the possibility that with cause, a general Council would be empowered to depose a reigning pontiff. Pasquier notes that action was taken, at the Council of Constance, against Benedict XIII, who we have just mentioned and whose given name Pasquier teases out derisively: "Pierre de la Lune" (Peter Luna) to emphasize the antipope's "lunar" instability and inability to carry out his office.[22]

We have said that for the medieval perspective Scripture and theology were both seen as parts of law, and we have also noted that this attitude is evident in Pasquier's own understanding. The French Church ought to govern its own affairs so that they will not be left to be neglected by Rome and that French money will remain in the kingdom rather than being surrendered in servile fashion to Rome. It is well known that Pasquier became allied with a political tendency known as the *politiques*, who took this attitude that the French ecclesiastical establishment ought not to lose revenues to Rome when the monies could serve needs of the domestic church.[23] Pasquier invokes indirectly the familial structure in the Pauline Epistle to the Ephesians, ch. 5, using the exhortation to love, respect and recognize mutual need, with Christ at the head, as a metaphor for the fabric of French society. He insists that God wishes to be worshiped with universal recognition as "le père commun de nous tous" (universal father). Thus he underlines his conviction which he often repeats in his works, that religious divisions are bad, both for the wholesome fraternity of citizens in the divine plan and for the integral continuity of the State. While his capacity to embrace altérité (difference) will widen with experience, it is demonstrable here and elsewhere in the texts of Book III that Pasquier's caveats against religious diversity reveal him as considerably less tolerant than critics have tended to make him. We shall return to an analysis of Pasquier's tolerance, but for now let us continue to explore some few other examples of his pro-Gallican arguments with regard to Rome. He speaks a great deal about a principal arm of ecclesiastical efforts to influence the activities of French kings with regard to ecclesiastical affairs. In ch. 18 we see the efforts of Pope Jules II to excommunicate Louis XII, who Pasquier assures the reader was always a loyal son of the Church. A Council held at Tours overturned the papal efforts to censure Louis. Pasquier reiterates that papal censures and excommunications have no effect on French kings and have always been turned against the pontiff in favor of the king. Moreover, popes have everything to gain in being "en bon ménage avec nous." (On good terms with us, the French)

12. The Term "Huguenot" in Context

So far we have seen that Pasquier's discourse in Book III refers to the Roman Church and its historic expression in France, where it has taken on the name "Gallican," and has developed as a national form of the one universal Christian Church. Pasquier and his Gallican colleagues have made distinctions between the pope's spiritual supremacy, which they recognize and affirm in their texts while never defining the concept formally, and his temporal authority, which for them is nonexistent in French territory. But Pasquier also affirms categorically that the pope's "spiritual" recourse to excommunication is also without effect when he applies it to French kings. Thus Pasquier and his colleagues work out a national Catholic reformation of their own which limits papal power and allows the Paris Parliament to retain control, in the king's name, over French ecclesiastical affairs. Meantime the "Evangelicals" are adopting their own reformed ecclesiologies in response to the influence of Calvin, Luther and other "Protestant" reformers. In the 1590s at the appearance of Book III of the *Recherches*, while the terms "catholique" and "protestant" are used to define individuals and groups, it is still anachronistic to speak of the division of "Catholic" and "Protestant" "Churches" in the plural, as an established fact. Terms such as "ceux de la religion"(those of the religion), "évangeliques," and "huguenot" gain greater or less currency in efforts to articulate the increasingly pluralistic confessional landscape. Inventing and applying such words also divided citizens into armed camps, he laments.

In Book VIII, Pasquier discusses the term Huguenot and a number of related terms and places them in the historical context of the Wars of Religion. He tries to be factual, balanced and he is also anecdotal. He begins ch. 55, "Du mot, *Huguenot*" by associating this term with "the greatest misfortunes ("malheurs") that can befall a people, either by fortune or by discourse, who become caught up in pettiness over the meanings of words that express their preferences (partialitez)." By the appearance of Book VIII in which he meditates on the political and cultural significance of language, he has had time to consider the civil strife that, as in France, had divided other societies: the Italians had known the conflict between the Guelphes and the Ghibellines, and the English had suffered through the Wars of the Roses. He also recalls an older French conflict between the Armignacs and the Burgundians. Sometimes the recourse to labels can be ruinous for an entire country, Pasquier asserts, as happened in the case of the Italians, just mentioned. Ruin came to France, he declares, because of those who recklessly invented the terms "Huguenot" and "Papiste," that divided the country, undermined law and civil order, and had tragic consequences. Although he sees the rise of the Calvinist and Lutheran religions as the cause of the divisions, he fluctuates in placing blame. We shall see that by the end of this chapter he ascribes responsibility for the disorder to extremism on all sides of the confessional debate. But he pauses to consider some attributes of John Calvin.

Pasquier's narrative about Calvin is especially of interest. He is balanced and even complimentary. While he has noted in his correspondence that "Geneva" was "the source of all our troubles," he acknowledges Calvin's superior style in writing in French, a point with which later critics would ultimately agree, seeing the reformer as one of the creators of modern French prose. He also admires his biblical erudition. Pasquier offers direct though still relatively mild criticism of Calvin. He conjectures that, had Calvin chosen "la bonne voye" (the right path) he might have emerged as one of the greatest of the doctors of the Church. He recognizes Calvin's zeal to promote his "secte." Pasquier conjectures that a great deal of insistent proselytism went on in French prisons where reformers or "ces pauvres gens abusez" as he calls them, were detained. He appears to say that they were unfortunate both for being detained but also for their subjection to regular visits by Calvin's messengers who constantly "exhorted, consoled and confirmed" them in the Reformed religion. He then notes that as the rank and file citizens took less umbrage at reformers, Calvin was encouraged to send a series of ministers or *predicans* into France. Pasquier shows neither empathy nor particular disapproval as he describes the condition of reformers who were reduced to worshipping in the new manner at night, in secret for fear of arrest.

Pasquier shares with his reader that since the term Huguenot has caused the country so much torment, he will be frank in giving his opinion of the events of when the term came into usage. The term Huguenot could be taken in various senses, he explains. Reformers who adopted it to describe themselves and who were opposed to the Guises who they suspected of trying to usurp the throne, identified with supposed forebears who had supported the Valois kings and who were descended from the line of Hugues Capet. Pasquier notes that there were many versions of how the term came into use. The first official notice of the word dates from 1559.[24] Henri II had launched a campaign against the heresies that the Huguenots had spread across the land, Pasquier recounts. He relates the campaign of suppression together with the execution of Anne du Bourg, by which the government hoped to intimidate other reformers. Following the word "Huguenot" in its historical context, Pasquier recounts the Amboise Conspiracy as key to the tumult that followed. There were opposing explanations for the plan to abduct the king, depending upon who one asked, Pasquier explains. At this earliest stage of the Wars of Religion, Reformers still felt loyalty to the crown, which was to be desacralized in their view after the outrages of the Ste. Bathelémy. But again, at this early stage of the religious drama, Pasquier seems to have no empathy for such clear lawbreakers who have tried to abduct the king. Not without cynicism he explains that "if one asks a Huguenot," the Amboise conspirators planned to "rescue" the young King François II from domination by the Guises, who they resented as usurpers of the guiding role, during the king's minority, which they felt should have been replaced by the princes of the blood, "whom the people naturally followed and loved," Pasquier qualifies. He characterizes the Huguenot conspirators as "mutins" (rebels) and asserts that this was the majority's opinion of them as well. We know that Pasquier also repeatedly returns to the perils that attend a king's minority, in his *Recherches de la France*. He dispassionately tells the reader about the consequent modes of execution of the conspirators but does not linger over this as a moral lesson as does d'Aubigné, in his *Sa vie à ses enfants*. In his discussion of the term Huguenot and how it was applied by the factions, he has occasion to consider other similar polarizing terms that sprang up during the confessional crisis.

Ch. 55 of Book VIII of the *Recherches* ends with a consideration of other terms that, similarly to "Huguenot" described the polarized conditions of the Wars of Religion and which undermined stability and the rule of established law.

As the term "Huguenot" was given to refer to many of the reformers, large numbers of whom had been captured in Tours, Pasquier explains, the name *Huguenot* spread throughout France. With it appeared the opposing name of *papiste*, or later, *catholique*. Pasquier uses the metaphor of a nursery of seedlings: from the word *catholique* sprang up other troublesome sub-categories: *catholiques associez*, as well as *catholiques mal contens*. Pasquier's own leanings came to be represented by the Catholic sub-category called *politique*, as is well known. He would spend the balance of the Wars of Religion and of his own career calling for the principle of peaceful coexistence between Catholics and Protestants, as we shall see illustrated shortly in his occasional poem, "Congratulation au Roy pour la Paix." The well-known *ligueurs* with much self-interest, opposed efforts at coexistence as contrary to their notion of the tenets of the Catholic religion, and efforts at cohabitation under the king provoked their continuous violent opposition. Pasquier counts four sub-categories of these: the *ligueurs zélés*, who wanted to eradicate both the Catholic *Politiques* and the *Huguenots;* there were also the *ligueurs espagnols*, who wished to see France ruled by the Spanish king or by the *Infanta*, his daughter. Still another category of *ligueur* wanted to exterminate the Reformed confessions but without at the same time provoking the ruin of the French State as it existed. Pasquier closes his chapter supposing that divine providence has deemed it necessary to trouble minds and the kingdom in this way.

I now return us to the final chs. of Book III, where Pasquier gives a full account of the Jesuits and their efforts to be integrated into the system of the University of Paris. In Book III, ch. 42, Pasquier focuses on the Jesuits referring to them as he had to Calvinists and Lutherans, as a "sect." Although the Jesuits are a *bona fide* Catholic religious order approved of by Rome and appreciated as educators and preachers popularly as well as by many prelates and indeed by other, regional *parlements* in many parts of France, we know that Pasquier and his fellow parliamentarians in Paris found it expedient to oppose them, as he notes, as subversive of the State. As Fragonard and Roudaut note in their critical edition of the *Recherches*,[25] in Book III, 42, he features a reprint of the text of his original trial brief in defense of the University of Paris against the Jesuits. In my chapters on his construction of his career and public *persona* as well as on the reception of his works I analyze his reasons for opposing the Jesuits, whom, notably, his close friend Pierre Pithou admired for their erudition and pedagogy.[26] Pasquier has come down to us, very similarly to Michel de l'Hospital as a voice of religious tolerance *avant la lettre*. However this characterization is not complete and would tend to divorce him anachronistically from the polemical and even invective side of debate in the later sixteenth century. Both men had a vested interest in maintaining public order under the firm hand of parliament, and both had recourse to the full panoply of rhetorical resources needed to persuade to their own *parti pris*. Invective was an aspect of the polemical rhetoric of the time that Pasquier, almost surprisingly, did not hesitate to deploy for his ends.

For the sake of demonstrating even more clearly than is already apparent in his narrative about the Jesuits in Book III Pasquier's strongly *intolerant* tendency, one needs to take into account his *Catéchisme des jésuites*, which was a work of no small sensation as demonstrated by the multiple printings and translations that appeared regularly, well into the seventeenth century. Claude Sutto's Critical Edition[27] remains the standard reference for this work which appeared for the first time from publisher Guillaume Grenier in Villefranche in 1602. Dorothy Thickett notes that Pasquier had trouble publishing the *Catéchisme*. She cites Jesuit father Louis Richeome in his own, anti-Pasquier work, *Chasse du renard Pasquier* (1603), in which Richeome accuses him causing discord and division among Christians and of having had his *catéchisme* published by Protestant printers in La Rochelle. Thickett further cites a contemporary letter from Neville, the English ambassador to France, to Lord William Cecil Lord Burghley, informing him that although the Nuncio had stopped the book's publication, Pasquier was asking to have it published in England, "bearing the name of Douay or some other place."[28] We know that the book was a publishing success in Protestant countries, as opposed to Catholic ones.[29] Claude Sutto's superb edition already mentioned remains the reference for Pasquier's use of the ambient invective, *ad hominem* and other, which show his lesser-explored, more ruthlessly *intolerant* side in the maintenance of his *persona*, as we have discussed, and in the service of Parliament's own self-interest, which was at times in marked contradiction to that of the king's own views or the climate of popular opinion, in this particular regard, to the Jesuits and their status in France.

· 5 ·

PASQUIER'S RECEPTION IN POSTERITY

1. Under the *Ancien Régime*, the Nineteenth and Twentieth Centuries

In most of his writings Pasquier makes it clear that he wanted to instruct future generations in what he found important to preserve in French law, ethics, customs and values. In the nineteenth century, Sainte-Beuve confirms that his reception in *postertité* was for Pasquier, a chief concern.[1]

The "handless" portrait Pasquier commissioned of himself during the *Grands Jours* at Poitiers from the artist De Hoey was calculated by him to celebrate his probity as a lawyer, and we have already discussed that image in the context of Pasquier's ever-conscious construction of his public persona. The De Hoey portrait can also stand as a metaphor for the prestige Pasquier enjoyed, for the most part, as evidenced by the many editions that were produced in the sixteenth and seventeenth centuries, notably the in-folio edition by the Thrévoux Press. We are aware of the negative response he received from Père Garasse[2] which was countered by his son, Nicolas Pasquier, and analyzed, first by Dorothy Thickett, if only in a somewhat perfunctory way in her annotated editions and more recently by

Denise Carabin.[3] (Garasse's hostility was no doubt partially a response to Pasquier's, and the Parliament's own anti-Jesuit invective, which ignored the important contributions of the Jesuits throughout France and their popularity with the people and with the French Catholic hierarchy.)[4] Indeed the only exception to the Jesuits' good reception in France was the Parliament of Paris, who saw them as an *ultramontaine* threat to their own power and influence. Pasquier, who was always conscious of how best to construct his own reputation and advancement with the Parliament, was an ambitious neophyte lawyer who used the strategy of supporting the powerful and influential University, which opposed the Jesuits' efforts to secure the right to teach within its structures, as it had earlier opposed the Dominicans. One can agree with the consensus of critics that his dislike of the Jesuits was genuine; however this seemed to soften with time.[5] Pierre Pithou, equally respected by his parliamentary colleagues, praised the Jesuits as cultivated and excellent pedagogues. The text of Pasquier's case against the Jesuits, however, is always included in subsequent editions of the *Recherches de la France*. Dorothy Thickett gives an exhaustive record of the editions including in translation into the other European languages, of an allied document by Pasquier, *The Catéchisme des jésuites*.[6] In addition, there was a mediocre reception to the reedition of Pasquier's *Recherches* that appeared in 1665.[7] Thickett notes various personages who owned copies of the *Lettres* in the 17th and 18th centuries, though the only edition to appear, in 1723, was the sumptuously bound two-volume edition of Pasquier's *oeuvres* by the Trévoux press.

Voltaire gives only a brief mention to Pasquier in his history of the Parliament of Paris. Saint-Beuve, who was the first modern literary critic to approach his work, finds him a mediocre poet, his prose lacking in vitality, this especially in regard to his writings on literature in the famous Book VII of his *Recherches de la France*.[8] We can be drawn to agree with Saint-Beuve particularly in regard to the mentioned Book VII of the *Recherches*, given our modern notions of literary criticism. Pasquier often seems more concerned with an author's, or with his work's, ethical and moral contributions to society than he ever is with aesthetic principles. But an exhaustive reading of his works will not fail to show the vividly colored flavor of his Middle French idiom, and this is true in all of his writings I believe, in both prose and verse. If attention paid to Pasquier during the time of the *Lumières* was sparse, a renewed enthusiasm for Early Modern authors in the nineteenth century worked in Pasquier's favor.

2. The Chancellor Pasquier's Edition of the *Institutes de Justinian*

In 1847 Etienne Pasquier's descendant, Etienne-Denis, duc de Pasquier, Chancellor of France, authorized the publication of Etienne Pasquier's *L'Interpretation des Institutes de Justinian: avec la conférence de chasque paragraphe aux ordonnances royaux, arrestz de parlement et coustumes générales de la France*, edited and with an introduction by Charles Giraud, who was himself a member of the *Académie des sciences morales et politiques*. We see then that Etienne Pasquier's self-portrait for emulation by his parliamentarian colleagues was carried on in posterity by others, who themselves wanted to construct their names in association with those of the illustrious past.

Etienne-Denis, duc de Pasquier was born in 1767 and like his ancestor, Etienne Pasquier, served in the Parliament of Paris. This Pasquier witnessed the tensions that developed between the Parliament and Louis XVI, until 1789 when Parliament was dissolved. Etienne-Denis left public life but was arrested momentarily under the Terror. He was released and restored to his property at the Thermidorian Reaction in July 1794. In 1809 he was created a baron of the Empire and prefect of Police. At the Restoration, Louis XVIII invested him as keeper of the Seal. Later, under the July Monarchy, he was created a duke, was elected to the Académie Française, and became Chancellor of France, when we find him presenting Etienne Pasquier's *Interprétation* to the public in this first and only publication. With the fall of Louis-Philippe Pasquier definitively left public life and focused on composing his memoirs.[9] Thus In 1847 chancellor Etienne-Denis Pasquier is at the height of his reputation. He further constructs his own *gloire* on the broad shoulders of the venerated Etienne in his rhetorically elegant *avant-propos* to Girard's edition of the *Interprétation*.

The tone of Chancellor Pasquier's *avant-propos* suggests that his remarks were likely presented initially in a speech, at a sort of "unveiling" of Etienne Pasquier's work, of which the chancellor is so proud and with which he wishes to demonstrate his personal, familial association, indeed, his ownership. His intention to identify with the text is seen from the outset: he desires to share the text with the public—a point on which Etienne Pasquier had always insisted himself—that he was a *zélateur du bien public*. The Chancellor adopts this same tone and says he is thus only fulfilling his duty (*mon* devoir). It would seem that the carefully chosen editor, the illustrious Giraud is the Chancellor's personal agent for his glory). He characterizes Giraud as one of the *lumières* of their time, a man of proven *gravitas*, equal to the *tâche* (task) a word employed with an air of a great undertaking, and the chancellor ardently testifies to "*toute la gratitude que je lui dois*" (all the gratitude that I owe him). The accentuated "je" actually eclipses in importance the editor, the text, and the (generous) act of "sharing" the same, with the public. The *topoi* of *captatio benevolentiae* as well as the disclaimer of one's own ability are seen in Etienne-Denis's momentary "doubt" as to whether he has anything worth adding—without *mérite*—to so valuable a work, but quite predictably, there comes a "*cependant*" (however) and he thinks that he will be able to say something, after all. It is a question here of a "méditation" on "Etienne Pasquier *and* "des érudits, et des jurisconsultes, ses contemporains" (Etienne Pasquier and the scholars and jurists, his contemporaries).[10] Thus he identifies the earlier Pasquier as a center of the legal class to which he himself belongs. *Méditation* is a word the chancellor chooses carefully for the purpose of exhorting the reader (or listener) now to consider matters of great moment, that is, great achievements of a singularly gifted legal historian and ethicist of the past, in the setting of his peers, and who give valuable example for the present and the future. They have made much progress in the science of historical investigation and in legislation, and the nation is duly grateful to them, Duc Pasquier asserts. He explains that he acquired the *Interprétation de Institutes* as a gift to him from a M. Dupin, to whom we shall return in this chapter. The chancellor characterizes Dupin as procurer-general and a magistrate who was *zélé* for the *gloire de nos anciens magistrats*, and so we can see that a new volley of propaganda favorable to parliamentarians was "in the air" in the late 1840s, largely constructed by themselves, as legists worked to support the struggling Orléanist regime much the way their judicial forebears had done in favor of the Capetian, the Valois and the Bourbon dynasties. Dupin's enthusiasm is an inspiration and an occasion for the Chancellor to identify with his still-prestigious ancestor. He wants this work by Etienne Pasquier which has never yet been published to be put to only the worthiest use.

Chancellor Pasquier then exhorts his readers to consider the excellent conditions that promoted literary activity in the time of Etienne Pasquier and his colleagues, when the pleasures of life focused for everyone in their own *foyer*, and there was, per force, ample time for meditation and scholarly pursuits. This focus is harder to come by in his own day he laments: the organization and progress of civilization, with greater facility in travel have brought with them many distractions that make such a focus on erudition much more challenging. The succession of French kings who reigned during

Etienne Pasquier's lifetime is considered. Pasquier was born in 1529 under François I and died in 1615 under Louis XIII. The chancellor briefly considers the assasination of Henri III and then, with more pathos, that of "France's best loved ruler, Henri IV," ". . . le grand roi . . . qu'elle a pleuré si longtemps . . ." (the great king . . . for whom she (France) mourned so long . . .) Under Louis XIII, the "scepter" had "so to speak, fallen into the hands of" Richelieu (who guided the State). These remarks about Pasquier's kings support Etienne Denis's thesis that jurists of the stamp of Etienne Pasquier and his peers had always been needed. They were a "classe éclairée de savants jurisconsultes doctes, et venerables" (an enlightened class of venerable and learned jurists." They were "infatigable" in their work and they *are "encore de nos jours l'objet d'une vive admiration.")* *"They are to this day the object of profound admiration."* And so Etienne-Denis emphasizes in effect that the portrait for emulation that Etienne Pasquier had so painstakingly fashioned of himself was still of influence in the ideals of Frenchmen of his generation. He echos the Aristotelian maxim, from the *Ars Rhetorica*, that the good orator must also be a good individual. He affirms that this was the case for Pasquier and his parliamentary peers. He invites the reader to an appreciation of their virtues, both public and private "which suppose an exacting use of their work days, which stretched far into the night." The chancellor goes on to avow that such diligent scholars and public servants were, like everyone, in need of a social life and relaxation; however they always lived as "gens de bien, en gens de beacoup d'esprit," and one might surmise the chancellor to see them as mid-nineteenth century descendants of the "honnête homme" that had begun to merge in sensibilities at the time in the pastoral works of Honoré d'Urfé, he himself an admirer and correspondent of Etienne Pasquier. The chancellor goes on to note that what social pleasures these men took were done with moderation, with the support of each other's cultivated company.[11] They supported each other in the *troubles* of the Civil Wars of Religion: "on trouverait difficilement un exemple plus frappant de cet heureux emploi des facultés de l'esprit, sinon pour echapper aux penibles emotions des tempetes politiques, du moins pour menager les forces dont l'homme de coeur a besoin, dans les agitations des discords civiles." (Only with difficulty could one find such a striking example of that happy use of the faculties of the mind, if not to escape from the difficult emotions of the political storms, at least to garner the strength which a sensitive man (homme de coeur) needs in the upheavals of the civil conflicts.)[12] Thus Etienne-Denis describes the image of a virtuous community strengthened against socio-politico-religious conflict, which was to stretch on through nine successive civil wars.

Only those who cultivate "letters" can know the reassurance and salutary diversion that are to be found in them, he asserts.

The virtues described above also provided these careful students of law with a strong sense of what constitutes the just and the unjust. Perhaps as a conscious reflection of having read Etienne Pasquier's famous letter to his son Theodore on the virtues of a good lawyer,[13] he praises the law and the legal profession which assures the 'triumph" of justice over inequity which would like to destroy it utterly (la immoler). He thus personifies these qualities. Pursued with "conscience," he continues, the study of law "raises and rectifies one's ideas" and "communicates to the soul the high morality that the science itself tries to apply to all civil interactions."[14] The chancellor insists that the legal efforts of these colleagues bore fruit as never before, and that they fought continually against "faction" and "disorder." An ideal allegorical scene of the ethical life is thus painted very similarly to that which Etienne Pasquier himself always portrays in his own writings. There is usually very little allowance in Etienne Pasquier's writings, for the possibility of jurists falling short of the ideal, and here there is only the hint of the antagonist's presence in the play. Chancellor Pasquier refers to "cette glorieuse phalange"[15] and exhorts his public to recall that they stood against the *Ligue* and prepared Paris to receive "le meilleur des rois qui aient gouverné la France." (the best of kings to have governed France [Henri IV]).

Having delivered a general *encomium* of the Paris parliamentarians as a body, the Chancellor then returns to Etienne Pasquier in particular, who, he assures, played his role in that "parti." He was one of those "honnêtes gens" who triumphed because of "bon sens" and "modération." In triumph, Etienne Pasquier's heart was the most magnanimous. He, like Henri IV was part of the "school of Michel de l'Hospital," the chancellor asserts, filled with high intelligence and the principles of wise tolerance. Thus one chancellor of France identifies himself with *the* iconic one, the most honored of names. He notes that in rejoining his parliamentarian colleagues, Etienne Pasquier felt no bitterness that they had not followed his path[16] but "only joy" to find himself again at the heart of the "grande famille judiciare ou il avait conquis, par son merite, une si grande et si belle place." ("The great judicial family where he had earned by his merits, such a great and honorable place.") With the metaphor of a storm and clouds that have lifted, Etienne-Denis notes that they in their own generation had come through together by good sense and fidelity to their prince. Much in the vein of Etienne Pasquier, he links their times with the upheavals that his own contemporaries have experienced: ". . . nous qui avons, aussi, vu de mauvais jours . . ." (the Revolution with the Terror and its wars, and the Napoleonic era.) The chancellor designated Charles Giraud, himself well known and a member of the Académie Française, to write an introduction to the volume of which he is also the actual publisher, while Chancellor Etienne-Denis Pasquier is the honoree.

Giraud gives one of the best, most readable and helpfully detailed accounts of Etienne Pasquier's life and career that I have seen, and he adopts the same politically fashionable encomiastic style and tone used by the chancellor in his *avant-propos*. This style, though not to our modern taste, serves Etienne-Denis and his own parliamentarian colleagues to emphasize to the public that Parliament's values, especially its leadership in government, are still necessary and will always continue to be so in the future. Thus his goals in publishing the *Institutes* are identical to Etienne Pasquier's own. The latter is called upon as a prime representative of everything that Giraud and the chancellor find virtuous and good from the legal wisdom of the sixteenth century. He cites Etienne Pasquier's own nostalgia for a climate of serious and careful studies that he benefitted from in his youth, and which is now waning in public education, as he has grown older. Studies were superior in Etienne Pasquier's day and by this implication, they ought to be renewed, in the 1840s. But above all, Pasquier represents the virtues of the legal profession, which at his time, Giraud asserts, lead to the highest honors. He gives a list of the most distinguished legal families, all of whom were known to Pasquier and he goes on to describe their relationships:

"Les mêmes moeurs, la même simplicité, la même dignité, régnaient dans la magistrature et le bareau. L'un était la pépinière de l'autre, et les relations les plus intimes existaient entre les deux ordres, dont les habitudes privées rappelaient les plus nobles exemples de l'antiquité. Loisel en a consacré la mémoire dans un ouvrage célèbre, qu'à l'imitation des anciens, il a intitulé du nom de *Pasquier, ou Dialogue des Avocats*, comme pour personnifier, dans ce seul nom, la plus belle époque que sa plume pût offrir à l'admiration du barreau moderne." (The same life-style, the same simplicity and dignity was to be found in the Magistracy and in the Bar. One was the seedbed for the other, and the best relations existed between the two groups, whose personal conduct recalled the noblest examples from antiquity. Loisel captured their memory in a well-known work, imitated from the ancients, entitled: *Pasquier, or The Lawyers' Dialogue*, as though to personify, with this one name, the finest epoch that his pen could offer as an example for the modern legal establishment.)[17] Giraud uses Loisel's descriptions, in the latter's book, *Pasquier ou dialogue des avocats*, to suggest a parallel with the judiciary of his own time. He wants to suggest that the current legal establishment is worthy of "la plus belle époque." In addition Giraud mentions one Matthieu Chartier, "devant lequel Pasquier rapporta son premier procès," (before whom Pasquier defended his first case),[18] and who was descended from the family of "the famous" Alain Chartier, for whom Etienne Pasquier had high esteem. Giraud notes that Loisel has Pasquier describe Matthieu Chartier in his *Dialogue des avocats*, as the moral center of the Parliament in his time, as he will portray Etienne Pasquier in the role as his *Dialogue* advances.

In the 1840s then, Pasquier's name was still well known, which can indicate that his works were still in circulation among *la classe dirigeante*. Giraud's *encomium* demonstrates a desire, at least on the part of some, to use Pasquier's name as a sure, reliable symbol of the ideals that the Magistracy and the Bar during the July Monarchy wanted to attribute to themselves. They were to find further support from a bibliophile professor and editor in Paris.

3. Léon Feugère and the "Selected Works" Series

In 1849 Léon Feugère, a professor of rhetoric at the Lycée Louis Le Grand, published his two-volume *Oeuvres choisies d'Etienne Pasquier*. Feugère's work on Pasquier is known to Giraud and he mentions him at the end of his introduction to the *Interprétation*. The editions by Giraud, Feugère and also Claude Dupin's edition of Loisel's *Dialogue des avocats* are the only works by, or about Etienne Pasquier that appeared in the nineteenth century. Feugère was a specialist in the editing of works of sixteenth-century French authors, notably Henri Estienne, Montaigne and Marie De Gournay, d'Aubigné, as well as Plutarch. He edited "selections," of various authors, in the case of Pasquier, "oeuvres choisies" (*Selected Works*). Feugère explains his rationale for publishing in his *avant-propos* to his edition of Pasquier. Perhaps in a manner that echos sentiments expressed by Etienne Pasquier himself, who, as we have seen, broadens the meaning of the term *chevalier,* Feugère esteems that the great "hommes de la paix" (makers of peace) should take their rightful place of honor beside France's military geniuses: with Turenne, Luxembourg and Condé, the nation ought to pay homage to Molé, Du Harlay, de Thou, and as this volume suggests, Etienne Pasquier. The nation gains from a renewal of their memory, Feugère declares.

Pasquier has been unjustly denied much credit as one of the artisans of French prose, Feugère argues. He alludes to unjust criticisms that have been leveled at him; and he insists that it will suffice to know Pasquier's texts to dissipate these. Feugère acknowledges that Pasquier had been duly noted as a *savant* but not as an écrivain (writer). His erudition was so admirable that it distracted critics from applying much focus on his literary style. Like Giraud and Chancellor Etienne-Denis Pasquier, Feugère makes reference to the Jesuits and thus joins in the ambient anti-Jesuit propaganda that was acceptable to the nineteenth century Paris Parliament. Feugère notes the "hateful" criticism that has overshadowed Pasquier in a veiled reference to the work of Fr. Garasse and other anti-Pasquier works by Jesuits, who were responding after all, in large measure to Pasquier's own free use of invective against the Society of Jesus. Such a tack was a strategy which he had judged as helpful to advance his legal career. Thus Feugère inflames the reader's indignation as he alludes indirectly to Jesuit "passions haineuses" (hateful passions) they had leveled against Pasquier, which had kept his works from being better appreciated. While Jesuits had certainly been critical in the past, Feugère, like Giraud perhaps, finds his advantage in encouraging an on-going political mythos of a valiant, anti-Jesuit Pasquier, symbolic protector of the rights of the Paris Parliament against *ultramontaine* interference in French affairs. In the same period, paradoxically, Pasquier's works were to be found in Jesuit libraries. They may have been stocked there for polemical reasons, but perhaps also because *Les Recherches de la France* had been known since the 1560s as a reliable source for the history of French institutions and culture, and such sources may have been useful and valued by the Jesuits in their educational and catechetical work. Feugère is complicit with parliamentarians when he aids them in spreading the perception that "today" all citizens enjoy a "common law and equal justice," and that it is no longer a question, in France, of splintered political parties or of opposing "banners." Thus Feugère facilitates Pasquier's reception by a new public, by editing his two-volume edition, which was appreciated by the general public of the time.

Feugère views Pasquier's work as a *mine* of information, but he focuses on him as a superior artist in prose, a quality which he demonstrates from excerpts of the *Recherches de la France* as well as the published *Correspondence*. To edit the entire *corpus* of his work would be frighteningly prohibitive for people of his times characterized by "peu d'efforts" (little effort), he explains. He therefore makes a selection from his works as from those of other authors, contemporaries of Pasquier he has edited, and he chooses what he finds to be "most valuable and durable." Perhaps echoing Pasquier himself, in *Recherches*, Book I in the chapters on the Gauls, Feugère urges the necessity of saving the "best efforts" of the writers of the nation's past for the sake of posterity. He notes that in regard to such "trésors" (treasures) "il faut se montrer le guardian zélé" (one has to assume the guardianship of such treasures with great zeal). The adjective "zélé" is of course derivative of the substantive "zélateur," of ambient use in the period and of which we have seen Pasquier make frequent use in describing the quality of his own efforts, in his writings and in his career, for the preservation of French values for the public good. Thus like the Duke Pasquier and Giraud, Feugère mirrors Pasquier's own thought and usage. Feugère concludes his *Avant-propos*, noting that he has opted for a modernized orthography for Pasquier's texts, in the interest of making them more approachable for the general reader and especially for foreigners. This latter point reflects that by the 1840s, editions of Pasquier's works had found their way to a wide range of European and North American libraries. He also notes that none of Pasquier's works had as yet been the object of critical editions, and that he has made an admittedly halting but hopefully a welcome effort to supply notes and commentaries, throughout.

Feugère makes the choice to include Pasquier among those authors of the sixteenth century worth editing in their own right, and he also includes him in an anthology of the period. He essentially continues to reiterate contemporary parliamentarian biases and *partis-pris* we have already seen in the writings of Giraud. For Dupin too, Pasquier was iconographic. He will press Pasquier's texts and appeal into a similar service of official propaganda, not without an essentially personal goal of self-fashioning of his own, as he simply adopts and amplifies many of Pasquier's own opinions and personal characteristics in his *Eloge d'Etienne Pasquier*, given at the 1843 opening of *Cour de Cassation* (High Court of Appeals).

4. Maître Dupin as "Alter-Pasquier"

The text of Dupin's *Eloge d'Etienne Pasquier* is included by Feugère in the second volume of his *Oeuvres choisies*, of which we have just spoken. Dupin adopts the Senecan axiom that one should look for a good and wise man as one's mentor and keep his eyes fixed on him as if to see what the sage would do in any given situation. Dupin does this in regard to Pasquier, and we shall see that his remarks in large measure are practically identical with those of

Pasquier himself. As Dupin opens his speech before the *Cour de Cassation*, the text of which he has been careful to preserve in print, he reminds his public that Pasquier is worthy to be placed among "les grands noms" (The great names) that "J'ai déjà évoqué" (I have already evoked), and thus he insinuates himself among their ranks as one worthy to invoke them. For him, Pasquier is among "les hommes célèbres qui *nous* ont précédés." (the famous men who came before "us.") Echoing the Horacian maxim that literature should both instruct and entertain, he praises him for writings and example which "intéressent," "profitent" and "instruisent." ("interest, profit and instruct"). He appraises that Pasquier and his contemporaries were of a superior stamp to those of his own day. Dupin gives relevant points of Pasquier's biography. He studied at the "antique et célèbre Université de Paris." If instruction was then less comprehensive or enlightened than in his time, Dupin asserts, students worked harder and were less distracted. He shows Pasquier's legal training, under Cujas and Alciatus, as well as his early experience of the bar, as ideals for all young lawyers who want to succeed according to the exigencies of the Paris Parliament, which includes the care for serious studies. Pasquier had prepared himself well in that regard during his lengthy two-year convalescence from mushroom poisoning. He acknowledges with respect Pasquier's *Recherches de la France* and his *Pourparlers*, as well as his "willingness," though still young, at age 36, to defend the University of Paris in the famous case against the Jesuits. Dupin then puts aside his direct focus on Pasquier to revisit that case. In black and white terms he praises the University while hammering the Jesuits over the next ten pages of his text. The University is "le creuset de toutes les saines doctrines" (the crucible of all sound doctrines); while he associates the Jesuits with "dissentions," "le schisme" and "les déchirements de nos guerres civiles." We recall that Pasquier himself had seen the Civil Wars of Religion, Calvin, Luther and the Jesuits all as so many subversive elements that ran contrary to the guiding wisdom of the Paris Parliament. Pasquier and parliamentarians had at length come to terms with all these *nouveautez* with the exception of the Jesuits who he and his descendant, the Duc Pasquier, Giraud, Feugère and Dupin continued to target, albeit the Order gained the support of Henri IV and was ultimately integrated into French society despite three historic expulsions, and today continues to operate its own schools and universities in France. Dupin's choice of Pasquier as a topic in part allows him to engage in a contrived and "pharisaical" anti-Jesuit discourse, which was still a safe staple of Parliamentarian propaganda at his time, and a strategy which no doubt served his professional assent, as it had served Pasquier's own.

In the vehemence of his discourse against the Jesuits, Dupin becomes an *alter*-Pasquier in that, on the strength of his mastery of rhetoric he perpetuates Pasquier's strategy of creating a popular perception of the University of Paris as the bastion of *Gallican* Catholic orthodoxy and the guardian, with the Parliament itself, of the very security of the State against a most insidious foe. It is important then, first for Pasquier's Parliament and later, for Dupin's, that the Jesuits be perceived not simply as a new, upstart teaching Order that desired to open schools and award degrees but as *ultramontaine* and subversive, *the* formidable enemy of the State itself. The truth then becomes less important than for Dupin to deploy the power of rhetoric to recreate the desired perception of a still eminent menace. Thus Parliament and University and Dupin, cast in Pasquier's own previous image and strategy, can shine as larger than life in their "victory," hailed as saviors of king and country, profiting to reassert the perception of their own power and prestige.

Once Dupin has made full use of what by then had become the *topos* of Jesuits-as-menace, he turns his attention to other aspects of Pasquier's life and career. He mentions the *Pourparlers* and the *Recherches de la France* as very significant, carefully prepared works. Dupin notes that "le style de Pasquier a souvent ce charme de naîveté qu'on trouve dans ses contemporains, Amyot et Montaigne. Peut-être meme se croyait-il superieur à celui-ci, auquel il reproche ses *locutions gasconnes*, rendant du reste grande justice à son esprit, et n'ayant, dit-il, nul livre entre ses mains tant caressé que les *Essais?*"[19] (Pasquier's style often features that naïve charm that one also finds in works of his contemporaries, Amyot and Montaigne. Perhaps he even felt himself superior to him, and he reproaches him for his Gascon locutions. He is just in identifying Montaigne's greatness of mind. He declares that he enjoyed no book more than the *Essays*.) Dupin gives a few more words assessing Pasquier's style: "on ne trouve dans aucun de nos prosateurs un style plus piquant, plus animé, plus richement semé de traits naîfs, d'expressions saillantes, de tournures tour à tour pleines d'abandon ou d'énergie, et de phrases qu'on aime à citer en texte, parce qu'on ne pourrait les traduire en d'autres termes sans en altérer ou en affaiblir le sens."[20] (In none of our authors in prose do we find so sharp, spicy and lively a style, one so richly sewn with naïve or strident expressions, with turns that are in places full of abandon and at others quite energetic, as well as lines that one enjoys so much to cite, directly from the text to avoid changing or weakening their meaning.) Dupin asserts that although Pasquier sometimes emphasizes small, unimportant points, and that much of what he wrote has (even at Dupin's own time) passed into popular culture,

Pasquier deserves full credit for having first assembled the materials he thought necessary to awaken the nation to the greatness of its institutions and culture. He always invokes him to personify the honor of the Parliament and of the *bareau*, underlining the Court's characteristic bravery in defending justice, even when to do so might prove dangerous. With this goal in mind he cites one such case of Pasquier's, that in which he defended the city of Angoulême in the latter's assertion that it was only defending its traditional privileges, and that it had not been guilty of treason against the king.[21] Dupin notes the prestige that accrued to Pasquier during his participation in the *Grands Jours* at Poitiers. Pasquier and his few fellow Parliamentarians who were able escaped Paris during the siege by the *Ligue* and loyally joined Henri III at Tours where they set up a government in exile. Thus Parliament is seen as intrinsically inseparable from the royal person and royal authority. Pasquier had also defended the honor of Lawyers in joining a general act of resignation when his colleagues refused to reveal publicly, on edict, the recompense they received from defending clients.[22] Dupin also gives high credit to Antoine Loisel for his narrative work: *Pasquier ou dialogue des advocats du parlement de Paris*, in which his main character, Pasquier, is the moral center of the court at his time, as he expounds with *gravitas* on the canon of Parisian legists of the past, and as he is surrounded by lifelong colleagues and friends, themselves also illustrious, particularly the same Loisel, and Pierre Pithou.[23] Perhaps a good summary of Dupin's *Eloge* of Pasquier may be seen in his qualification that Pasquier served his king, not as a courtier but as a magistrate, that the best service he could offer was to help the king to know and defend established, customary law, and not simply to comply with flights of royal self-interest.

5. Sainte-Beuve

The voice of literary criticism in the 1840s and 50s could not help but turn his attention to Pasquier's merits, this was of course Sainte-Beuve, who had a similar agenda in writing to that which had been Pasquier's own: his *causeries du lundi* were a strategy to build fame and a reputation for aesthetic discernment for himself, and also to educate the public in morals and politics.[24] He writes on the cusp of the new school of *L'art pour l'art*, and the Horacian principle for authors still holds sway, though at the same time, part of Sainte-Beuve's appeal for us remains his willingness to critique points of style or image on purely esthetic grounds. Refreshingly, he is not afraid to critique more extensively

Pasquier's merits, and to recognize in his work certain artistic shortcomings or limitations of perception.

In his article "Etienne Pasquier" in volume 3 of *Causeries du lundi*, Sainte-Beuve acknowledges his awareness of the Chancellor Pasquier's edition of The *Interpretation des Institutes de Justinian*, and he seems to follow the lines of Charles Giraud's excellent introduction, at least partially as a guide for his own critical approach. He also shows admiration for Feugère's *Oeuvres choisies*. He repeats many of the comments about Pasquier and his work that we have noted in these works and in Dupin. It appears clear that the attention Pasquier's memory has received on such high levels has had something to do with Sainte-Beuve's own decision to do a feature on him, and he has also familiarized himself to some extent with the main lines of *Les Recherches de la France* as well as with something of Pasquier's correspondence and his French poetry. He also claims some acquaintance with his Latin verse. All of his sources on Pasquier may well come from the works of Giraud and Feugère, the latter of whose edition he carefully describes.

For Sainte-Beuve, Pasquier was no original thinker, not one ahead of his time like Montaigne, Rabelais or Amyot, the last of these is normally placed "only with some complacency" with the great. Sainte-Beuve credits Pasquier as being among the period's . . . "quantité d'excellents et vigoureux esprits, de graves et énergiques personnages, qui usèrent vaillamment ou sainement des resources de la langue à cette époque de confusion et de lutte, et qui, en l'appliquant selon des besoins divers, y mirent encore moins l'empreinte de leur génie propre que celle du parti et de la classe auxquels ils appartenaient." (a number of excellent and vigorous minds, grave and energetic personages who used courageously and wisely the resources of language during a time of such confusion and struggle, and whose efforts reflected not so much their own spirit as that of their particular party or social class.)[25] He asserts then that Pasquier represented the views and habits of his fellow parliamentarians. He represented the spirit and exceptionally respectable tone of the magistrature of his time. Sainte-Beuve notes that Pasquier's poetry, similar to that of others of his legal peers, shows wit and elegance but no real originality. Was St. Beuve aware of Pasquier's association with Ronsard, and that he subscribed to the *Pléïade's* doctrine on imitation? He congratulates him for having chosen to express himself in French, in his *Recherches*, which he qualifies as "doctes et utiles," in much of his poetry and in his correspondence, which, mistakenly, Sainte-Beuve believes him to be the first to have published such a collection in France. He credits him with being among the first to realize that French experience *which was never Roman* ought not to be expressed in Latin but in the national vernacular. Pasquier is steeped in Latinity, and so is hardly opposed to it, but he is more given to composing in his mother tongue. Sainte-Beuve notes that for Pasquier the purity of the French language is found not in the heavy language of the legal system, nor in the "effeminate" idiom of the Royal court, but a bit everywhere in France, among ordinary people. As for his prose style, Sainte-Beuve has this to say: "Son style est de robe longue, même dans ses lettres où il ne vise point à être pompeux; mais, à tout moment, il rachète ses défaults réels, ses longueurs de phrase, par des expressions heureuses qui honororaient Montaigne. Il joint à sa gravité habituelle, à la justesse et à la prud'homie de ses pensées, un agrément qui sent la poésie dans la prose. Ce reste de poëte, insuffisant dans la pure poésie, revient à point pour égayer et comme pour fleurir ses pages sérieuses."[26] (His style is that of a judge, even in his letters where he has no desire to be pompous, but he regularly makes up for his real defects, such as his too-lengthy sentences, by agreeable turns of phrase that would even honor Montaigne. Joined to his habitual *gravitas*, precision and balance of thought there is a pleasurable impression of poetry being created in prose. This sort of trait of the poet, which would not be enough in pure poetry, appears in turns to lighten and beautify his serious pages.)

St. Beuve's choice of Pasquier for incorporation into his *Causeries de lundi*, as a significant figure in literary and judicial history testifies to Pasquier's continued currency among the fashionable, general reading public in the nineteenth century. This suggests that Pasquier was thus still in vogue, and not simply among law students and parliamentarians, and that to publish at least a selection of his works was still regarded as a viable editorial option. However, apart from St. Beuve's efforts and the single, 1848 printing of Feugère's *Oeuvres choisies*, there were no subsequent editions of Pasquier's works for the remainder of the century.

6. The Twentieth Century

Pasquier would be relatively neglected from the late nineteenth century until studies conducted by Dorothy Thickett in the 1950s–70s. Thickett published critical editions of much of his correspondence, a very useful bibliography, which includes Pasquier's printed editions and remaining known manuscripts, as well as anonymous occasional pieces and foreign translations of some of his works. She later produced a lively and well-written biography[27] based on the correspondence. Thickett's groundbreaking work remains indispensable as a reference for Pasquier scholarship. Clark Keating produced a concise biography in 1972. A fine critical edition of *Les Recherches de la France*, by Marie-Madeleine Fragonard and François Roudaut appeared in 1996.[28] Useful colloquium papers were published by the *Cahiers Saulnier* in 1991[29] and included some rapprochements in methodology with Voltaire and the *philosophes*—But today Pasquier is read for the most part only by historians of historiography and by literary antiquarians. Moreover, Pasquier is still absent from many encyclopedic works on sixteenth century authors that have appeared in current times. There have been a number of dissertations about Pasquier's *Correspondence* or his works overall, as well as my own dissertation on Pasquier's use of history to teach ethics, and also shorter works on his life or some aspect of his work, the latter focusing also chiefly on his role as a historian. He remains relatively neglected by scholars, similarly to other key figures of their time, notably Claude de Seyssel.[30] One important exception to this tendancy is the extensive and inciteful work on Pasquier done by Catherine Magnien[31] and the team that composed the 1996 Critical Edition of Pasquier's *Recherches de la France*. As conferences in the field of Early Modern Studies turn to the examination of figures thought of until now as "secondary"—such as was the lot of Pasquier until very recently—more important work will be devoted to Pasquier's contribution to the dynamics of the period of the Wars of Religion and their aftermath in terms of the development of political, religious and literary values.

· 6 ·
CONCLUSIONS

Etienne Pasquier was in every sense an exponent of the Parliament of Paris. He and his colleagues shared a desire to provide a modern history of France, its customs and laws, to serve as a permanent guide and a moral compass for the continuity of France as an autonomous state in the future, especially in troubled times such as their own. To this end the *robins* had also drawn up the first written account of the *Coutume de Paris*. Pasquier and all the parliamentarians we have mentioned, including Christophe and Jacques de Thou and others had collected and edited early manuscripts, as well as charts, and other documents to produce the materials for a responsible history of France approaching our modern criteria for historiography, though history was still subordinated by the writers to their own exigencies. Pasquier reflects this activity of doing instructive, exemplary history in his *Recherches de la France*, which for the most part remains a still reliable account of the development of French national institutions. He publishes his *Correspondence* according to these same criteria and motivations, and in his letters, he encourages the reader to assemble the elements of his own character as model public servant. In another example of the parliamentarian's industry, Jacques de Thou also produced his multivolume *Historia sui Temporis*, and Henri de Mesme wrote his memoirs. All of this gathering of historical artifacts went to illustrate ethical guidelines for political, religious and social conduct.

Pasquier's wish to instruct future generations was realized. As we have seen from the *encomia* offered to the Parliament, in turns by Pasquier himself, as well as his descendant, the Chancellor Duke Pasquier, as well as Giraud and *Maître* Dupin, the *robins* saw themselves as guarantors of the King's authority—as arbitrated by themselves—and of continuity and security for their own times and for *posterité*. This self-concept of the Parliamentarians' role is echoed in all of Pasquier's own writings and in the actions he placed in constructing his life and career. Scévole de Sainte-Marthe, a sometime mayor of Poitiers, a poet and critic well respected among the *robins*, admired Pasquier's poetry, and the two were regular correspondents. Scévole's biographer , Roche-Maillet, names some of Scévole's key acquaintances, among which we note Pasquier and others of his own circle:

> Lors du séjour qu'il fit à Paris és années MD.LXIX & LXX. Il acquit encore la bien-veillance de Pontus de Thiard et de Guillaume Ruzé, qui furent depuis, l'un Evesque de Chalon en Bourgongne & l'autre d'Angers, de Germain Vaillant de Guellis Abbé de Pimpont, Conseiller en la Cour & depuis Evesque d'Orléans; de Christophle de Thou tres-digne premier Président de la Cour de Parlement; de Henry de Mesme Seigneur de Roissy, Conseiller d'Estat Chancellier de Navarre [. . .], Ils ont continue ceste affection au sieur de Sainte-Marthe; ce qu'ont fait aussi Guy du Faur Seigneur de Pibrac alors Advocat general du Roy, puis Président au Parlement de Paris, Philippe des Portes Abbé de Tyron, Estienne Pasquier Advocat du Roy en la Chambre des Comptes, Antoine l'Oisel, Pierre & François Pithou, celebres Advocats en la Cour.[1]

We can see that self-fashioning or self-construction was a pursuit shared by many illustrious figures. Among those named here: Pontus de Tyard, Christophe de Thou, Henry de Mesme, Pibrac, and Pasquier's more immediate friends, Loisel, Pierre Pithou and Pierre's brother, François. Pasquier's desire to be established as guide to the nation for the sake of continuity as well as his amplification of his desired image as defender against the invented enemy, the Jesuits, was integrated by his own generation of Parisan *robins* and by the French judicial establishment of both the Bourbon Restoration and the post-Second Empire Periods. It is also of interest that an image of Michel de l'Hospital now graces the façade of the Hôtel Bourbon, *siège* of the Fifth Republic's *National Assembly*. Thus the virtues enjoined by Pasquier and his colleagues on the public defense in their day are remembered in perpetuity.

Pasquier's *Pourparlers* have received little critical attention. These brief works, as all of his writings, develop, amplify or at times simply repeat the themes that we begin to recognize as we read through his works. As the

Pourparlers can be viewed as secondary pieces, much recycling of the material used in writing the on-going projects of his *Recherches*, or his *Correspondence* is predictable. This same tendency to *recyclage* characterizes of course the still more occasional pieces such as the *Congratulations* and other political verse. Themes such as national origins, the original superiority of the Gauls, especially in statecraft, in judicial affairs and in proto-French "national" ecclesiology recur. The characteristic virtues of male and female political leadership are regularly recognizable topics as well. Pasquier deploys the elements of the traditional *speculum principis* in the indirect advice he gives to the Queen Mother and to her sons, as well as to Henri IV. In the *Pourparlers* Pasquier adapts Platonic texts as they develop a discourse on the qualities of good government that is well prepared for. How best to prepare? There is a traditional discussion of what constitutes the best education for a prince. Ethics of penal justice incarceration and legitimate servitude are all discussed, and Pasquier also alludes to his knowledge of medicine and of anatomical studies. These themes and others held in common with the thinkers important at the time including Paracelsus, and also the poets of the *Pléïade* and more specifically with Ronsard, in his political poetry become *lieux communs* of the period. In addition, the *Pourparler de la loy* insists that the good citizen will obey the laws and customs of his own country. In a departure from the precepts of *Défense et illustration*, Pasquier values the lessons of medieval French history to instruct his own times, while simultaneously he prefers the trends in poetics of his own time, and he is also proud of France's continuous *renommée* in the realm of poetry since the earliest rise of the vernacular. The personages encountered by the reader in the *Pourparler du prince*, the *Pourparler de la loy* and in the *Pourparler d'Alexandre* are not at all an attempt on Pasquier's part at literary characterization but are "voices," or allegories for his manipulation of commonplace ideas about what constitutes just and effective royal government as well as conduct becoming *un bon français*. Perhaps one of the most interesting of these borrowed personages is that of Rabelais, whose works we know Pasquier enjoyed. More study would reveal interesting borrowings or transformations of Rabelais' material in Pasquier's own texts.

Pasquier's Book III of his *Recherches de la France* is a Gallican reaction to the phenomenon of the *Mutations de religions* as he styles them, a consequence of which were the nine successive Wars of Religion. The matter of security and continuity of France had become urgent. Pasquier reminds his reader in all of his major works and in occasional ones that nascent Lutheranism,

Calvinism and, for he and his parliamentarian colleagues, the presence of the Jesuits—were all causes of concern about the security of the State. For him these new movements were all "sects"; e.g., "le secte des jésuites." Of course the Protestant Churches had not yet been crystallized as such: Pasquier refers to "Luther," and to "Calvin" or to "Genève," or to "ceux de la religion." Indeed the word "religion" can be synonymous with undesirable but later tolerated "sects." He mentions "Huguenots," and has an article on this term in Book VIII of his *Recherches*. He never refers to "les réformés or to "la Réforme." Pasquier, who has been characterized by Dorothy Thickett as a rare voice of tolerance of diversity, was less tolerant than he was pragmatic. His pragmatism indeed sets him apart from many of his contemporaries. He is excessively intolerant at times, especially of the Jesuits against whom I find his ire thoroughly contrived and invented in accord with pressures from his fellow *robins*, who were resentful of the order's successful reception in France. In the *Catéchisme des jésuites* or in other of his anti-jesuit writings, even the erstwhile tolerant Pasquier deploys the ambient invective of the age, used by all the confessions to discredit each other.[2] The anti-Jesuit calculation was also of course amplified by Pithou and others in their satirical work against the *ligue*, *La Satire Ménippé* (1593). Despite implications put forward by critics Dorothy Thickett and George Huppert particularly, Pasquier was not a "Protestant" in spirit, indeed the term remains anachronistic for the time; nor was he an unbelieving positivist, or deconstuctionist, or a Voltaire *avant la lettre*, writing in favor of religion only for prudence's sake. We also have the internal evidence from his texts in the *Recherches* and from his correspondence that he identified as a believing Roman Catholic. Some of his unedited letters are really full-blown meditations on religion, and Thickett herself testifies to the existence of Pasquier's commentaries on the Gospels, now thought to be lost. His meditative tableaux about Jeanne d'Arc and Marie Stuart, both found in Book VI of the *Recherches*, serve as *exempla* for the reader, suggesting that religious conviction and service to one's country, given by God are not in contention. Pasquier through all this, though, was a *lay* Roman Catholic, not a cleric-theologian, and his training and his *lexicon* for articulating his thought are legal ones. Book III of his *Recherches*, whose vast erudition and the reflection it implies witnesses to his Catholic faith while it just as emphatically reminds that the Church in France is not and cannot be a *porte-parole* of the pope, but is and must remain an essential component of the French monarchy, in like manner as the other essential limbs of the body politic, the Parliament and the University. Eventually Pasquier moved beyond the sense of threat he felt implied by the presence of the Huguenots; his occasional political verse works from the early years of the reign of Henri IV to show that while he still recognizes Gallican Roman Catholicism and tolerates the Huguenots, the sense of abiding urgency about saving the State impels him to rebuke even the aged Cardinal Davy du Perron, Ronsard's eulogist, to put aside extremism in religion for the sake of national unity, and that as the very definition of the duty of the good citizen, who Pasquier enjoins to remain ever *un bon français*.

NOTES

Chapter 1: Introduction

1. Etienne Pasquier: *Les Oeuvres melées d' E. Pasquier*. A Paris: Chez Jean Petit-Pas, 1619.
2. Pontus de Tyard, 1522–1605, Pasquier's friend and correspondant, joined him in his support of Henri III against the *Ligue*. In his homilies, Tyard called for public order, with one united church and a clergy in on-going self-reform: Pontus de Tyard, *Oeuvres Complètes* vol. VI, critical edition by Marie-Madeleine Fragonard, François Rouget and François Roudaut. Paris: Champion, 2007, 15.
3. Paul Bouteiller. *Recherches sur la vie et la carrière d'Etienne Pasquier*. Paris: Editions ISI. 1989, 1–10.
4. Ibid., 6,7.
5. Catherine Magnien: "La FORTE GUERRE" d'Etienne Pasquier contre Ramus réformateur de l'orthographe dans les *lettres*: une fiction demonstrative," in: Kees Meerhoff, et al.: *Autour de Ramus le combat*. Paris: Champion, 2005. 405–426.
6. François Roudaut and Marie-Madeleine Fragonard produced a three-volume critical edition of the *Recherches*, with Champion in 1996. See also my *Etienne Pasquier on Ethics and History*, for a full account of this work.
7. Details cited in Etienne Pasquier, *Pourparlers*, critical edition by Béatrice Sayhi-Périgot. Paris: Champion, 1995, 9–10. Sayhi-Périgot also notes that the institution of the *Grands-Jours* disappeared by the middle of the seventeenth century.
8. Espiner-Scott, *Claude Fauchet, sa vie et son oeuvre*. Paris: Droz, 1938.
9. Pasquier: *Recherches de la France*, critical ed. by Roudaut and Fragonard, Paris: Champion, 1996: VII, 6, 1411.

10. Dahlinger, James H. : article "Jean Dorat" in *Dictionary of Literary Biography*. Vol. 327, *Sixteenth-Century French Writers*. Ed. Megan Conway. New York: Bruccoli Clark Layman, 2006.
11. Charles de Bovelles' *Liber de differentia vulgarium linguarum et Gallici sermonis varietate* was a major inspiration to Pasquier as he completed Book VIII of his *Recherches*. See note 7, p. 1497 in vol. III of Fragonard and Roudaut's Critical Edition of the *Recherches de la France*.
12. See the entry "Huguenot" in *Recherches* III, VIII, 1670–1674.
13. Hospital, "Discours au Parlement de Paris pour la convocation des Etats-Généraux et du concile" (7 septembre, 1560) in: *L'Hospital: Discours pour la majorité de Charles IX*, 45–58.
14. See Timothy J. Reiss, *Knowledge, Discovery and Imagination in Early Modern Europe* for a discussion of the concept of continuity in the sixteenth century, 2–4.
15. George Huppert, *The Idea of Perfect History*.
16. Pithou, Pierre: *Les Libertés de l'église gallicane*, 1594.
17. Dorothy Thickett explains that Pasquier towards the end of his career wrote commentaries on the Gospels, which are thought not to be extant today. *Estienne Pasquier the Versatile Barrister of Sixteenth-Century France*, p. 20.
18. Dorothy Thickett, *Bibliographie des oeuvres d'Estienne Pasquier*. Geveva: Droz, 1956. 152–153.

Chapter 2: Pasquier's Self-Fashioning as the Ideal Public Servant

1. I presented a partial version of this chapter as a paper, at the Sixteenth Century Studies Conference, 2009. Greenblatt, Stephen. *Renaissance Self-Fashioning*. Chicago: University of Chicago Press, 1980; Jardine, Lisa. *Erasmus, Man of Letters*. Princeton University Press, 1993.
2. Pasquier, *lettres familières*. Letter 3, Book XI, 189, to his son, Pierre Pasquier.
3. Two famous exceptions to this norm are Guillaume Budé and Jacques Cujas.
4. See also my *Etienne Pasquier on Ethics and History*, ch. 3, "Pasquier and His Colleagues of the Parliament of Paris."
5. Pasquier. Lettres familières. Lettre VI to Theodore on the profession of being a lawyer, 157–163; To Pierre, Book XVI, letter V. 254–55.
6. Same as note 2, pp. 37–45.
7. Michel Beaujour, *Miroirs d'encre*, Paris: Seuil, 1980, 5–13.
8. Geertz quoted in Stephen Greenblatt: *Renaissance Self-fashioning*. 3
9. Ibid., 4.
10. Etienne Pasquier. *Lettres familières*. Ed. Dorothy Thickett, Geneva. Droz, 1974. Livre VIII, lettre 1 à Monsieur Pithou, Seigneur de Savoye Procureur-Général du Roy en la Chambre de Justice en Guyenne. 125–135.
11. Ibid., 126–127.
12. Emma Cayley. *Debate and Dialogue: Alain Chartier in His Cultural Context*. Oxford: Clarendon Press, 49 ; Pasquier. *Lettres familières*, ed. D. Thickett. Book VIII letter 1 to Pithou: a card game from the 14th century. Thickett's note 12, 134.

13. Etienne Pasquier. *Recherches de la France*, IV, 31, 989–990. Pasquier describes the maneuvers of chess as a metaphor for the maintenance of the king's position and authority in the State.
14. For the circumstances of the *Puce*, see my *Etienne Pasquier on Ethics and History*, 28–29; also Kendall B. Tarte, *Writing Places*. University of Delaware Press, 2007; Anne R. Larsen. Ed. and trans. *From Mother and Daughter: Poems, Dialogues and Letters of Les Dames Des Roches*. Chicago: University of Chicago Press. 2009.
15. See the article *oisiveté*, V. Krause. *Dictionnaire de Montaigne*. Ed. Philippe Desan. Paris. Champion, 2007. 836. While Pasquier avoids idleness as he embarks on his career at the *Palais*, Montaigne for his part has entered upon retirement as he reflects in his essay, *De l'Oisiveté* on the perils but also on the fertile possibilities of allowing the mind to wander unimpeded. For Villey this brief essay suggests the genesis of the writing project for Montaigne, and I would suggest that a similar dynamic is at work for Pasquier (who we know read the *Essais*), in the gradual elaboration, editing and polishing of his *Recherches de la France*.
16. Pasquier, *Lettres familières*, Book 8, letter 1 to Pithou, 127.
17. Unlike the case of the youthful Guillaume Budé who we know was fond of falconry, and who "wasted" much of his youth with friends before settling into his prodigious itinerary in studies. Guillaume Budé: *De Transitu Hellenismi ad Christianismum*. Ed. Maurice Lebel. with modern French translation, Sherbrooke, Éditions Paulines, 1973, introduction, xiii–xv.
18. Same reference as note 14.
19. Treated also by Erasmus, See Emile Telle, *Erasme de Rotterdam et le septième sacrament, Etude d'évangélisme matrimonial au XVIe siècle et contribution à la bibliographie intellectuelle d'Erasme*, Geneva: Droz, 1954. Cited in *Philologie et subjectivité, ed.* Dominique de Courcelles, Paris: Ecole des Chartes, 2002. 84–85.
20. Pasquier, *lettres familières*, Ed. Dorothy Thickett. Book 1, letter 9 to Germain Le Picard. 20.
21. Ibid., Book 2, letter 5, 45.
22. Ibid.
23. Though nothing authorizes us to say that Pasquier's character was marked strongly by either of these traits. he nonetheless thought himself a good judge of character, as he narrates in his successful defense of the Sieur d'Arconville. He was able to discern innocence from the composure he saw on the young man's face.
24. See Dahlinger, *Etienne Pasquier on Ethics and History*. 31.
25. Pasquier, *Lettres familières*. Book 6, letter 1 to Scévole de Sainte-Marthe.
26. Ibid. *Recherches de la France*, Book II, 19, 503–508, for queen regents; Book VI, 2, 1121–1125; Book VI, 2, 1125–1145 for the troubles that threaten during a king's minority; similar troubles at the *démence* of Charles VI, respectively.
27. Cited in *Les Oeuvres melees d'Etienne Pasquier*, Paris: chez Jean Le Petit Pas, 1619.
28. Final part of the same letter cited above, to Pithou.
29. There have been recent efforts to rehabilitate a received negative view of the Cardinal de Lorraine: See Jean Belsamo. "Le Cardinal de Lorraine et l'académie remensis," in Christian Mouchel and Colette Nativel, ed.: *République des lettres, république des arts*. Geneva: Droz, 2008. 13–36. Mouchel and Nativel focus on the cardinal's many educational initiatives, including his support of two Jesuit institutions.

30. Pasquier. *Lettres familières*. Ed. Dorothy Thickett. Book II, letter 1, to the Cardinal de Lorraine. 20–23.
31. Pasquier was very attached to the Guises, a point which also partially explains this *dedication* to Charles de Lorraine. He also dedicates chapter 15, Book VI of his *Recherches de la France* to a narrative about the last days of Marie Stuart, also a Guise. (Fragonard and Roudaut. 1219–1228.)
32. Final part of the same letter to Pithou, cited in note 17.
33. *Lettres familières*, liminal letter to Loisel. 1.
34. Lisa Jardine. *Erasmus, Man of Letters*. Princeton University Press. 27–53.
35. I reproduce this latter portrait with permission, in my *Etienne Pasquier on Ethics and History*.
36. Letter to Theodore, *Lettres familières*, 156–163.
37. Philppe Desan. *Portraits à l'essai: iconographie de* Montaigne. Paris: Champion, 2007. 13–18.
38. See my *Etienne Pasquier on Ethics and History*.
39. Philippe Desan: *Portraits à l'essai*. 62, 70.
40. Ibid., 11.
41. Catherine Magnien."La 'Forte Guerre' de Etienne Pasquier contre Ramus;" in *Autour de Ramus, le combat*. Ed. Kees Meerhoff et al. Paris: Champion, 2005. 405–425.
42. Loisel's most well-known work, *Pasquier ou dialogue des avocats de Paris* lists the lawyers of the Paris Parliament from 1524 to 1599. It was republished by Dupin in an edition of the correspondence of Camus in two volumes in 1818. (The details about Loisel's life featured in the above paragraph are borrowed from Michaud, *Bibliothèque Universelle*, Akademische Druch U. Verlagsanstalt, Graz: Austria, 1968, Vol. 25, 34–35.) Interestingly enough, this article mentions Pithou and Cujas, but not Pasquier, though the series does feature a three-page article on him.
43. Pasquier, *Lettres familières*, Book I, letter 1, p. 3, to Loisel.
44. Ronsard spoke of the moral and civic virtues, in his "Institution pour l'adolescence du roy très Chrestien Charles dixieme de ce Nom."
45. We find the tradition of a cart and chains as a sign of shameful criminality most famously in Chrétien de Troyes' *Lancelot, ou le chevalier de la charette*.
46. See the account of Arconville's trial Pasquier provides in Book XII, letter 1 to Espesse: *Lettres familières*, ed. D. Thickett, 202–208.
47. William V. Bangert, SJ. *A History of the Society of Jesus*. Revised edition. Saint Louis: The Institute of Jesuit Sources, 1986. 64–71.
48. For the Jesuit case and others that helped to define Pasquier's career, see my *Etienne Pasquier on Ethics and History*, as well as my chapter on Pasquier's *fortune*, in the present work.
49. See Dorothy Thickett's permanently useful *Bibliographie des oeuvres d'Estienne Pasquier*, Geneva, Droz. 1956, 122–152, for the many French and also foreign language editions of the *Catéchisme des jésuites* and related pieces by Pasquier or attributed to him.
50. Theodore was beneficiary of his father's post in the magistracy and in the *Cour des comptes*; Pierre was a captain in the royal military. See my *Etienne Pasquier on Ethics and History*, 50.
51. Nicolas Pasquier, *Le Gentilhomme*. Ed.Denise Carabin. Paris: Champion, 2003.
52. Ibid., 153.

Chapter 3: Law, Custom and the Individual, Revisited in The *Pourparlers*

1. The *disputatio*, a didactic, pedagogical exercise, always survived in the universities and in general, in the French educational system since the medieval period. See Françoise Waquet, "La longue vie de la dispute: contribution à l'histoire d'un genre universitaire," 135–147 in *République des lettres, république des arts*. Geneva: Droz, 2008.
2. That is, until the critical edition by Béatrice Sayhi-Périgot: *Pourparlers*. Paris: Champion, 1995. All references to the *Pourparlers* are from Sayhi-Périgot's edition. Note also other articles on the *Pourparler du prince:* John Parkin: "Etienne Pasquier: Tolérant ou indécis?" *Studi Francesi* 24 (May–August 1980): 225–33; "Machiavellism in Etienne Pasquier's *Pourparler du prince*." *Modern Language Review* 68 (July 1973): 530–44.
3. The *Pourparler du prince* appeared with the first edition of Book I of Pasquier's *Recherches*, by Sonnius, in 1560.
4. Robert Descimon, ed., *L'Hospital, discours pour la majorité de Charles IX*. Paris: Imprimerie Nationale, 1993. See also, Thierry Wanegffelen; *De Michel de l'Hospital à l'Edit de Nantes: Politique et religion face aux églises*. Presses Universitaires Blaise-Pascal, 2002.
5. Etienne Pasquier: *Lettres historiques*. Book IV, letter 6, to Christophe de Fonssomme. Ed. Dorothy Thickett. Paris: Droz, 1966, 51.
6. Montaigne: *Essais:* Book I, ch.23: "De la coustume, et de ne changer aisément une loy receüe." Ed. Villey, Quadrige, PUF, new edition, 1988.
7. For Pasquier's sonnet addressed to Pibrac, see James H. Dahlinger: *Etienne Pasquier on Ethics and History*. New York: Peter Lang, 2007, 1–6.
8. See first note of this chapter.
9. Etienne Pasquier, *Lettres historiques*, Book IV, letter 3 to Christophe de Fonssomme. Ed. Dorothy Thickett, Paris: Droz, 1966. 31–32.
10. Jean-H. Mariéjol: *Catherine de Médicis*. Paris: Librairie Jules Tallandier, 1979, 98.
11. Etienne Pasquier, *Lettres historiques*, Book IV, letter 10, to Fonssomme, 65.
12. Pasquier outlines the importance that a people keep a written record of their culture for *posterité* in the introductory matter and in the chapters on the Gauls, in Book I of his *Recherches de la France*. See also James H. Dahlinger: *Etienne Pasquier on Ethics and History*, New York: Peter Lang, 2007, 53–55.
13. *Curial* is a term Pasquier employs with some regularity, here as well as in his *Recherches*.In the *Pourparler du prince* he notes that the word is one he has adopted "de nos vieux poètes français" (perhaps from Alain Chartier, who Pasquier mentions with esteem and who authored a satirical work on the court, *De Vita Curiali*, to which we shall return). William Calin: *The French Tradition and the Literature of Medieval England*.Toronto: University of Toronto Press, 1994, 250.
14. Du Bellay composed the Pléïade's manifesto, *la Défense et illustration de la langue francoyse*, in 1549. Pasquier, who agreed with much of Du Bellay's contents has his *Escolier* state that the king should be the model of the educated Frenchman whose conduct is informed by literary and cultural values.
15. In a letter to Antoine Loisel, Pasquier explains that he finds it natural to express his thoughts in his native language, French, while he also composes some Latin verse. Cicero too, he

argues, wrote most often in Latin, his native language, and less often in Greek. Etienne Pasquier: *Lettres familières*, ed. Dorothy Thickett, Paris: Droz, 1974. Book I, letter 1, 3.

16. Guillaume Budé: *De l'institution du prince*. Farnborough Hants, England: Gregg Press Limited, 1966.
17. Ibid.
18. Courtizan:1560–1594: Curial: 1596 to 1723. Pasquier. *Pourparlers* ed. Béatrice Sayhi-Périgot, 54, note 1.
19. Sayhi-Périgot explains that what immediately follows is a borrowing from Cicero's *First paradox*: Etienne Pasquier. *Pourparlers*, Béatrice Sayhi-Périgot, ed. 61, note 7.
20. Pasquier: *Les Recherches de la France*, Book VII, ch 3. 1388. Pasquier seems to have been quite familiar with the *Roman de la Rose*, which he explains constituted a compendium of moral philosophy, and a text illustrating the virtues and the vices in the course of its narrative.
21. Sayhi-Périgot's critical edition of the *Pourparlers*, note 48, 118.
22. Pasquier, *Recherches*, Book IV, ch 5, 894 and following.
23. Ibid., Book II, ch. 17. 479–483. Pasquier criticizes those who enjoy a noble ancestry and its privileges without actually serving at arms, or at least in public service of the State. Anyone who lives an upright life of service is "noble," he declares, but the tradition of honors and hereditary distinctions has to be recognized and maintained.
24. Pasquier: *Pourparlers*, Sayhi-Périgot's critical edition, note 55, 120.
25. Ibid., note 62, 121, though the reference is readily recognizable.
26. Etienne Pasquier, *Lettres historiques*. Ed. Dorothy Thickett, Droz, 1966. Book IV, letter 1, to Fonssomme. Pasquier laments the Italian Wars, which he admits have brought more harm than good to France.
27. Montaigne: *Les Essais*. ed. Pierre Villey. Paris: Quadrige, PUF, 1965. Vol. 1: "Qu'il ne faut juger de nostre heur,Qu'apres la mort." Did Pasquier have this essay in mind as he writes the part of the *Philosophe* in the *Pourparler du prince*? Though the ideas were ambiatory at the time, the same need for equanimity of spirit and a well-ordered life is discussed in both works.
28. *Recherches* books I and VIII join a vogue for etymological studies promoted, among others, by Henri Estienne.
29. Ibid., Book IV, chs. 5,6,7.
30. *Pourparler du prince*, 76.
31. *Pourparler du prince*, 83.
32. Guillaume Budé: *De L'Institution du prince*. Ed. Farmborough Hants, England: Gregg Press Ltd., 1966.
33. The term chatouilleuse (delicate, difficult) Is one Pasquier likes to use and which he may be consciously borrowing from his reading of Rabelais, though the term is current throughout the XVIth century.
34. On Giovio, (1486–1552) see also Pasquier, *Recherches de la France*, Book I, ch 3. 259, Fragonard and Roudaut.
35. Burckhart tried to restore Giovio's reputation as a reliable historian, followed by T.C. Zimmerman: *Paulo Giovio: The Historian and the Crisis of Sixteenth Century Italy*. Princeton University Press, 1995.
36. On the tendency to falsify antiquities in the sixteenth century see: Ginette Vagenheim: "Pirro Ligorio et l'Accademia Degli Sdegnati," in Deramaix, Marc et al., eds., *Les Académies dans l'Europe Humaniste*. Geneva: Droz, 2008,108–109.

37. Aristole: *The Art of Rhetoric*. Trans. J. H. Freese. Loeb Classical Library. Harvard University Press, 1991.
38. *Recherches de la France*, Book I, Introduction.
39. On the title page of Budé's *De Transitu Hellenismi ad Christianismum* we read the aphorism: 'Garde-toi d'avoir une haute opinion de toi-même." French translation of this work with facing Latin text, *De l'Hellenisme au Christianisme*, by Maurice Lebel. Sherbrooke: Éditions Paulines, 1973.
40. *Pourparler*, 94.
41. Like Pasquier himself, Claude Seyssel has been relatively neglected by the critics. See Rebecca Ard Boone, *War, Domination and the Monarchy of France: Claude de Seyssel and the Language of Politics in the Renaissance*. Leiden: Brill, 2007.
42. Béatrice Sayhi-Périgot: *Pourparlers*. 159, notes 183–187.
43. Marie-Dominique LeGrand. Le *Traité de la reformation de la justice* et les idées "politiques" de Michel de l'Hospital, in Thierry Wanegffelen, ed. *De Michel de l'Hospital à l'édit Nantes*. P.U. Blaise-Pascal, 2002. 279–287.
44. Dorothy Thickett. *Bibliographie des oeuvres d'Estienne Pasquier*. Geneva: Droz, 1956. The *Pourparler de la loy* was published also by Gilles Robinot in 1596 and by Laurent Sonnius in 1607. In each case, the three *Pourparlers* accompany these new editions of the *Recherches*.
45. Timothy Reiss. *The Meaning of Literature*. Ithaca: Cornell University Press, 1992.
46. Philippe Desan. *Dictionnaire de Michel de Montaigne*. Paris: Champion, 2007, 1060–1061.
47. Sayhi-Périgot, note p 47, p. 117 on the prominence in Pasquier's time, of La Boétie's *Discours de la servitude volontaire*.
48. Erasmus, *In Praise of Folly*,and More, the *Utopia*. As noted by Sayhi-Périgot, 109.
49. *Recherches*, IV, I, 2; Sayhi-Périgot, 168.
50. Pasquier's remarks about women, in his various writings range from the ambient misogyny, to the *gallant* and the Petrachan, to a shrewd awareness of their influence and how to avail himself of this, to respect for their intellectual or political achievements.
51. Pasquier joined the medical discussions of his day. He shares his own interest in the field, and comments on the historical worthies of the medical profession, in his *Correspondence*: See letter XVI, to Tounèbe, Dorothy Thickett, ed., Pasquier's *Lettres familières*, 304–311; 322.
52. Sayhi, note 16. 186.
53. Frank Lestrigant has edited a number of Thevet's geographical texts, notably: *Histoire d'André Thevet Angoumoisin, Cosmographe du Roy, de deux voyages par luy faits aux Indes Australes, et Occidentales*. (co-edited with Jean-Claude Laborie. Geneva: Droz, 2006).
54. See *Recherches* II, 1, 322. In a discussion of the aftermath of the fall of Rome, France alone had remained intact and had escaped rule by foreign powers: "Nous seuls, qui avions comme les autres, trouvés nostre grandeur dans les despoüilles de Rome, sommes demeurez redoutez et florissans jusqu'à huy, sans avoir enduré la possession d'autres rois, que de ceux qui ont fait estat de la Gaule, comme de leur vraye séjour." (We alone. Unlike the other realms who found there grandeur in the ruins of Rome, we (alone) have remained feared and flourishing up to the present day, without having had to endure the rule of any kings other than our own, who made Gaul their true home.)
55. Pasquier admired Paraselsus. See *Lettres familières*, ed. Dorothy Thickett, Geneva: Droz, 128: Pasquier defended the "Paracelsistes" in a case against the Paris Faculty of Medecine; 303–310. He attempts a brief history of medicine in Book XIX, letter 16, to Tournebus.

56. Sayhi- Introduction to her critical edition of *Pourparlers*, p. 38
57. Michel de Certeau. *L'Ecriture de l'histoire*. Paris: Gallimard, 43.
58. Michel de Certeau notes historians' prejudice in favor of the humanists at the expense of the scholastics, in the introduction of his *Ecriture de l'histoire*.
59. Pasquier describes this tradition of the first of January in *Recherches* IV, 9, 918.
60. Cite Gauls and Francs, Caesar and Gaulish culture wiping out Charlemagne and blotting out other rulers' memory
61. Sayhi-Périgot: Pasquier's idea aller de soi, p. 39.
62. Certeau, M. de, his discussion of the politically and sociably *pensable*. Similar in style to the opposite English expression, "unthinkable!" What his public could receive was always foremost to Pasquier in deciding his agenda for writing. Certeau, *L'écriture de l'histoire*, Paris: Gallimard, 1975, 5.
63. There is extensive discussion of the categories of law: De jure naturali, gentium et civili" in Pasquier's *Interprétation des Institutes de Justinian*, ed. Charles Giraud, Paris: 1847, 18–26. The work remained unpublished until it came to the attention of the Chancellor Etienne-Denis Pasquier.

Chapter 4: Law and the Christian Tradition in France

1. Michel de Certeau. *L'Ecriture de l'histoire*. Paris: Gallimard, 1975. The idea of writing what is *pensable*, thinkable, or receivable by a culture or a social class, in this case, the Parisian parliamentary establishment. 47.
2. Pasquier. *Lettres familières*. Ed. Dorothy Thickett. Book VIII, letter 1, to Pierre Pithou. 127.
3. Pasquier. *Recherches* III, 8, 576.
4. Pasquier. *Recherches*, III, 7, 562. "...je ne me lasseray jamais de célébrer l'auctorité du Saint Siège de Rome..."; also: III, 17, 639.
5. Philippe Desan, ed. *Montaigne et la théologie*. Geneva: Droz, 2008, 7.
6. Pasquier. Lettres familières. Book 2, letter 9. 49–52. See also following note by Dorothy Thickett.
7. Dorothy Thickett. *Etienne Pasquier, the Versatile Barrister of Sixteenth-Century France*. London: Regency Press, 1979.
8. P. Bouteiller. "Historique et contenu des Recherches de la France d'Etienne Pasquier," in *Cahiers Saulnier, Etienne Pasquier et ses Recherches de la France*. Presses de l'Ecole Normale Supérieure. Paris, 1991.
9. Robert Descimon. *L'Hospital, discours pour la majorité de Charles IX*. Imprimerie Nationale, 1993, 7–8.
10. Jean Du Tillet. *Memoires sur les libertés de l'Eglise gallicane*; 639; Pithou. *Les libertez de l'Eglise Gallicane*, Lyon, Pierre Ponthus, 1771 edition; Claude Fauchet. *Traité des libertez de l'Eglise Gallicane*.
11. Pasquier. *Recherches* III, 16, 633–34.
12. Ibid.
13. Charles B. Schmitt and Quentin Skinner, eds., *The Cambridge History of Renaissance Philosophy*. Cambridge University Press, 1988. 114.

14. Erasmus. *The Education of a Christian Prince*. Translated and ed. Lester K. Born. New York, Octagon Books, 1973. 197.
15. Pasquier. *Recherches*. Book III, 2, 530.
16. George Huppert. "Pasquier Philosophe." In *Etienne Pasquier et ses Recherches de la France*, Cahiers Saulnier 8, etc.
17. Pasquier. *Recherches* III, Introduction, 513.
18. Pasquier. *Lettres familières*.Ed. Dorothy Thickett. Book II, letter 5, 41
19. Luc Racaut. *Hatred in Print*. Cornwall: Ashgate, 2002.
20. *Recherches* III, Introduction, p. 511.
21. Pasquier. *Recherches*. III, 12, 610.
22. In Book VII of his *Recherches de la France*, Pasquier praises the *Roman de la rose*, taking pleasure in Jean De Meung's focus on "moral philosophy." I am unaware whether Pasquier was familiar with Gerson's "Contre le Roman de la Rose," number 320 in the *Oeuvres complètes*, ed. Mgr. Glorieux. Tournai: Desclée, 1965, 301–316. Gerson condemns the "Rose" as contrary to Christian faith and morals.
23. *Recherches* III, 17, 638.
24. Fragonard and Roudaut's critical edition of the *Recherches*, VIII, 50, 1671, note 670.
25. *Recherches*, III, 42, 801.
26. See also my *Etienne Pasquier on Ethics and History*, p. 42.
27. Etienne Pasquier. *Le Catéchisme des jésuites*. Ed. Claude Sutto, Editions de l'Université de Sherbrooke, Quebec, 1982.
28. Dorothy Thickett. *Bibliographie des oeuvres d'Estienne Pasquier*. Geneva: Droz, 1956, 122.
29. Ibid.

Chapter 5: Pasquier's Reception in Posterity

1. Sainte-Beuve. *Causeries du lundi*. Paris: Garnier, 1852, III, 249.
2. Garasse. *Recherche des Recherches d'Estienne Pasquier*.
3. Nicolas Pasquier, *Le gentilhomme*. Ed. Denise Carabin. Paris, Champion, 2003.
4. William V. Bangert, S.J. A *History of the Society of Jesus*. Saint Louis: Institute of Jesuit Sources,1971.
5. Giraud, Introduction to Pasquier's *Institutes*.
6. D. Thickett. *Bibliographie des oeuvres d'Estienne Pasquier*. Geneva: Droz, 1956. 122–136.
7. Article on Trevoux in *Etienne Pasquier et ses Recherches de la France*, by Cahiers Saulnier.
8. Charles-Auguste de Sainte-Beuve. *Tableau historique et critique de la Poésie française et du théâtre français au seizième siècle* (Paris: Charpentier, 1869), 39; *Causeries du lundi*. Paris: Garnier, 1852, III, 257; both cited in Suzannne Trocmé Sweany, *Etienne Pasquier et nationalisme littéraire*. Paris: Champion, 1985; 13, 17.
9. *Histoire de mon temps: Mémoires du Chancellier Pasquier*; publiés par M. le duc d'Audiffret-Pasquier.
10. *Interpretation*, a.
11. Dorthy Thickett. *Etienne Pasquier the Versatile Barrister of Sixteenth Century France* explains that the legists lived and socialized in their own sections of Paris, in the Rue des Saints Pères.

12. *Interprétation*, page d.
13. Dorothy Thickett, ed. Letter of Pasquier to his son Theodore, in which he cites the law as one of the few professions, with that of clerics, allowing for the divine infusion of virtues into the soul.
14. My translation.
15. *Interprétation*, p. e.
16. Etienne-Denis Pasquier, *avant-propos:* 9.
17. *Interprétation*, viii. For an analysis of Loisel's *Pasquier ou dialogue*, see also my *Etienne Pasquier on Ethics and History*. New York: Peter Lang, 2007, 23; 33–36.
18. *Interprétation*, ix.
19. Cited in Dupin's text, p. 239.
20. Ibid., 239.
21. For the details of the case see the Trévoux edition or my *Etienne Pasquier on Ethics and History*, 43–44.
22. See my *Etienne Pasquier on Ethics and History*, 33–34.
23. Ibid., 22, 33–35.
24. Philippe-Joseph Salazar makes this latter point in an interesting article, "L'Ecrivain et la politique: Les causeries du lundi au fil des pensées," in *République des lettres, république des arts*. Eds. Christian Mouchel and Colette Nativel. Geneva: Droz, 2008, 601.
25. *Causeries*, 250.
26. Ibid., 257.
27. Dorothy Thickett. *Etienne Pasquier, the Versatile Barrister of Sixteenth-Century France*. London: Regency Press, 1979.
28. All of these works are listed in full in my bibliography.
29. Also cited in the bibliography.
30. Although a work has just appeared: Rebecca Ard Boone. *War, Domination and the Monarchy of France, Claude de Seyssel and the Language of Politics in the Renaissance*. Leiden: Brill, 2007.
31. Catherine Magnien's work is cited in the bibliography.

Chapter 6: Conclusions

1. Roche-Maillet, *Vie de Scévole de Saint-Marthe*, p. 198. Cited in the introduction, xxxvii, to *Scévole de Saint-Marthe, Oeuvres Complètes*, vol. 1, ed. Jean Brunel. Geneva: Droz, 2010.
2. See Luc Racaut, *Hatred in Print. Catholic Propaganda and Protestant Identity during the French Wars of Religion*; Claude Postel. *Traité des invectives au temps de la Réforme*.

BIBLIOGRAPHY

Primary Sources

Pasquier, Etienne. *Les Recherches de la France*. Critical Edition in 3 vols, Marie-Madeleine Fragonard and François Roudaut, Paris: Champion, 1996.

________ *Lettres familières*. Ed. Dorothy Thickett. Paris: Librairie Droz, 1974.

________ *Lettres historiques*. Ed. Dorothy Thickett. Paris: Librairie Droz, 1966.

________ *Oeuvres*, 2 vols. Amsterdam: Trévoux, 1723.

________ *Pourparlers*. Critical Edition by Béatrice Sayhi-Périgot, Paris: Champion, 1995.

________ *Oeuvres choisies*. Edition Léon Feugère, 2 vol. Firmin-Didot, 1848.

________ *Le Catéchisme des jésuites, ou examen de leur doctrine*. Paris: Guillaume Grenier, 1602.

________ *Le Catéchisme des jésuites ou examen de leur doctrine*. Sutto, Claude, ed. Sherbrooke, U, Sherbrooke, 1982.

________ *L'Interprétation des Institutes de Justinian*, Ed. Charles Giraud, Paris: Videcoq, 1847.

________ *La main ou Oeuvres poétiques faits sur la main de Estienne Pasquier*, Paris: A l'Enseigne de la Corne de Cerf. 1584

________ *Les Oeuvres d'Estienne Pasquier*. (2 vols) Ed. Trévoux, Amsterdam. 1723.

Pasquier, Nicolas. *Le gentilhomme*. Critical edition by Denise Carabin, Paris: Champion, 2003.

Secondary Sources

Aristotle. *The Art of Rhetoric*. Ed. John Nenry Freese. Harvard University Press, 1947.

Bangert, William V., S.J. *A History of the Society of Jesus*. Saint Louis. The Institute of Jesuit Sources. 1986.

Beaujour, Michel. *Miroirs d'encre*. Paris. Seuil, 1980.

Bohler, Danièle and Magnien-Simonin, Catherine. *Ecritures de l'histoire, (XIVe–XVI siècle)* Geneva. Droz, 2005.

Bouteiller, Paul. *Recherches sur la vie et la carrière d'Etienne Pasquier*. Paris. Editions ISI, 1989.

Bowen, Barbara C. *Humour and Humanism in the Renaissance*. Aldershot Hampshire. Ashgate, 2004.

Budé, Eugène de. *Vie de* Guillaume *Budé*. Paris. Émile Perrin, 1884.

Budé, Guillaume. *De Transitu Hellenismi ad Christianismum*. Sherbrooke. Éditions Paulines, 1973.

________ *De l'Institution du prince*. Ed. Farmborough Hants, England. Gregg Press ltd., 1966.

Cahiers V. P. Saulnier. *Etienne Pasquier et ses Recherches de la France*. Presses de l'Ecole Normale Supérieure. Paris, 1991.

Calin, William. *The French Tradition and the Literature of Medieval England*. Toronto. The University of Toronto Press, 1994.

Cave, Terrence. *The Cornucopian Text*. Oxford University Press, 2013.

Cayley, Emma. *Debate and Dialogue—Alain Chartier in His Cultural Context*. Oxford. Clarendon Press, 2006.

Certeau, Michel de. *L'Ecriture de l'histoire*. Paris. Gallimard, 1975.

Chartier, Alain. *Le Quadrilogue invectif*. E. Droz, ed. Paris. Champion, 1950.

Contamine, Philippe. *Des Pouvoirs en France, 1300–1500*. Paris. Presses de l'Ecole Normale Supérieure, 1992.

Courcelles, Dominique de. Ed. *Philologie et subjectivité*. Paris. Ecole des Chartes, 2002.

Dahlinger, James H. *Etienne Pasquier on Ethics and History*. New York. Peter Lang, 2007.

________ article, "Jean Dorat" in *Sixteenth-Century Writers; Dictionary of Literary Biography*. Ed. Megan Conway. New York. Bruccoli Clark Layman, 2006.

Demaizière, Colette. "Etienne Pasquier lecteur de Thibaut de Champagne," in *Thibaut de Champagne, prince et poète du XIIIe siècle*. Ed. Yvonne Bellenger and Danielle Quéruel. Lyon. La Manufacture, 1987.

Deramaix, Marc, Galland-Hallyn, Perrine, et al., eds.: *Les Académies dans l'Europe Humaniste*. Geneva. Droz. 2008.

Desan, Philippe. *Montaigne et la théologie*. Geneva. Droz, 2008.

________ *Portraits* à l'essai: *iconographie de Montaigne*. Paris, Champion, 2007.

________ *Dictionnaire de Michel de Montaigne*. Paris, Champion, 2007.

Descimon, Robert. *L'Hospital, Discours pour la majorité de Charles IX*. Paris. Imprimerie Nationale, 1993.

Espiner-Scott, *Claude Fauchet*: *sa vie et son oeuvre*. Paris. Droz, 1938.

Fouqueray, Henri, S.J. *Histoire de la Comagnie de Jésus en France*. (2 vols) Paris. Alphonse Picard et Fils, 1910.

Fragonard, Marie-Madeleine and Pierre E. Leroy. *Les Pithou: Les lettres et la paix du royaume*. Paris. Champion, 2003.

Fumaroli, Marc. *L'Age de l'eloquence*. Geneva. Droz, 1980.

Greenblatt, Stephen. *Renaissance Self-Fashioning*. Chicago. University of Chicago Press, 1980.

Huguet, Edmond, *Le Langage figuré au seizième siècle*. Paris. Hachette, 1933.

_______ *Dictionnaire de la langue française au seizième siècle*. Paris. 1925–1967

Huppert, George. *The Idea of Perfect History*. Urbana. University of Illinois Press, 1969.

Ignace, Saint. *Constitutions de la Compagnie de Jésus*. Paris. Desclée de Brouwer, 1967.

Jardine, Lisa. *Erasmus, Man of Letters*. Princeton. Princeton University Press, 1993.

La Croix-du-Maine et de Verdier. Tome 2. *Les bibliothèques françoises de la Croix-du-Maine et de Du Verdier*. Saillant et Nyon Paris, 1773.

Langer, Ulrich. *Rhétorique et intersubjectivité: Les Tragiques d'Agrippa d'Aubigné*. Paris. Papers on French Seventeenth Century Literature, 1983.

Larsen, Anne R. Ed. and trans. *From Mother and Daughter: Poems, Dialogues and Letters of Les Dames Des Roches*. Chicago. University of Chicago Press, 2006.

L'Ecrivain, Philippe. *Paris au temps d'Ignace de Loyola*. Ed. Facultés Jésuites de Paris, 2006.

Magnien, Catherine. "Etienne Pasquier "familier" de Montaigne?" *Montaigne Studies*. 13 (2001) pp. 277–313.

_______ "Estienne Pasquier Historien." *Revue du Seizième Siècle*. 19 (2001) pp. 51–62.

Margolin, Jean-Claude, ed. *Anthologie des Humanistes européens de la Renaissance*. Paris. Gallimard, 2007.

Meerhoff, Kees, Moisan, Jean-Claude and Magnien, Michel. *Autour de Ramus, le combat*. Paris. Champion, 2005.

Nativel, Colette. Ed. *Centuriae Latinae II Cent une figures humanistes de la Renaissance aux Lumières*.Geneva. Croz, 2006.

Périgot, Béatrice. *Dialectique et littérature: les avatars de la dispute entre Moyen Age et Renaissance*. Paris. Champion, 2005.

Pibrac, Guy du Faur de. *Les Quatrains et les plaisirs de la vie rustique*. Geneva. Droz, 2004.

Poncet, Olivier, and Storez-Brancourt, Isabelle. *Une histoire de la mémoire judiciaire*. Paris, Ecole Nationale des Chartes, 2009.

Postel, Claude. *Traité des Invectives au temps de la réforme*. Paris. Les Belles Lettres, 2004.

Potter, G. R. *The New Cambridge Modern History*: Vol I, *The Renaissance*. Cambridge. Cambridge University Press, 1967.

Racaut, Luc. *Hatred in Print*. Aldershot, Hants. England, 2002.

Reiss, Timothy J. *Knowledge, Discovery and Imagination in Early Modern Europe*. Cambridge University Press, 1997.

Rouget, François. *Ronsard et le livre*. Geneva, Droz, 2010.

Scévole de Sainte-Marthe. *Oeuvres Complètes*. vol I. Jean Brunel, ed. Geneva. Droz, 2010

Tarte, Kendall B. *Writing Places*. Newark. University of Delaware Press, 2007.

Thickett, Dorothy. *Bibliographie des oeuvres d'Estienne Pasquier*. Geneva. Droz. 1956.

_______ *Etienne Pasquier, the Versatile Barrister of Sixteenth-Century France*. London. Regency Press, 1979.

Tricotel, Edouard. *La Satire Ménippée*. Paris. Alphonse Lemerre, 1881.

Trocmé-Sweany, Suzanne. *Etienne Pasquier et le nationalisme littéraire*. Paris. Champion, 1985.

Vitz, Evelyn Birge. *Medieval Narrative and Modern Narratology*. New York. New York University Press, 1989.

Wanegffelen, Thierry, ed. *De Michel de l'Hospital à l'Edit de Nantes*. Paris. Presses Universitaires Blaise-Pascal, 2002

INDEX

Abbon, bishop of, 78
Acts of Parliament, 70
adversaries, construction of, 29–30
Agesilaus, 40
Alciatus, 97
Alençon, duke of, 28
Alexander the Great, 37, 39, 44, 47, 59, 60–64
alliances, 47
altérité, 49, 106
ambition, 59, 60, 61, 75, 77–78
Amboise Conspiracy, 6, 62, 83
Amyot, 98, 100
ancien régime, Pasquier's reception during the, 87–88
ancienneté, 5, 66, 68, 69, 72
Annales de France, 45
Antioch, 8
antiquitez, 5, 37–38
Apostles' Creed, 71
Apostolic Age, 7
archbishops, 70. *See also specific clergy*
Arconville, Sieur d', 29, 111n23
Argenteuil, 35
Aristotle, 51, 58
  Ars Rhetorica, 91
Aristyppus, 52
Armignacs, 82
Ars Rhetorica (Aristotle), 91
l'art pour l'art, 99
"Assemblée des Trois Estats Tenue en la Ville de Blois, 1588", 87–102
Aubigné, d', Agrippa, 94
Augustus, 37, 62

Bar, the, 4, 5, 94, 97, 99
barbarians, 55
Barthelémy, Saint, 62, 83
Baudouin, 3
Beatitudes, 8
Beaujour, Michel, 14
Béguin, grand maître du Collège du Cardinal Lemoine, 4
Belen, Françoise, 4, 19

Bellarmin, Robert, 69
Benedict XIII (antipope), 80
Berlanger, count of Provence, 37
bishops, 70, 78. *See also specific clergy*
Blanche of Castille, 22
Bloom, Harold, 10
Boétie, La, *Discours de la servitude volontaire*, 50
Boniface VIII, Pope, 38–39
books, making, 18–19
Bourbon Dynasty, 90
Bourbon Restoration, 89, 104
Bourg, Anne du, 83
Bourges, 28
Bouteiller, Paul, 2
Bovelles, Charles de, 5, 6
Brittany, 47
Budé, Guillaume, 24, 46, 111n17
  De l'Institution du prince, 37, 43
Burgundians, 82
Burgundy, 47

Caesar, Julius, 47, 62, 75
Cahiers Saulnier, 102
calculation, 61
Calvin, John, 82–83
Calvinism, 8, 30, 81–84, 97, 105–6
Capetian Dynasty, 90
Carabin, Denise, 88
Cardinals, 76
carnavalesque, 52
Catechism of the Council of Trent, 69
Catéchisme des Gallicans, 7, 71
Catéchisme des jésuites (Pasquier), 7, 85, 88, 106
  Pasquier, Etienne, 10, 30
Catherine de Médicis, 21–23, 25, 36, 60, 105
Catholic Reformation, 76, 81
Catholicism, 3, 6–8, 29–30, 65, 67, 73, 84–85, 88, 106. *See also* the Church
Catullus, 43
Causeries du lundi (Sainte-Beuve), 10, 99–101
Cayley, Emma, 17
Cecil, Robert, 85
Ceres, 42–43
Certeau, Michel de, 57, 61
Charlemagne, 60, 61, 74, 76, 77
Charles IV, 36
Charles V, 39, 47, 71
Charles VI, 47
Charles VIII, 43, 44
Charles IX, 62
Charles le Téméraire, 40
Charroulois, Charles de, 39
Chartier, Alain, 94
Chartier, Matthieu, 94
Chartres, Yves de, 66
Christ, 7, 8, 71, 72, 76
Christianity, 57. *See also* doctrine
  Eastern, 8
  French, 68
  law and, 65–85
  tradition of, 55
Christology, 8, 71, 75
Chronique du seigneur de Langey, 45
Church, the, 65, 66. *See also* clergy; doctrine
  disunion in, 73
  ecclesiastical ethics, 3
  Gallican, 2, 6–8, 31, 66, 68–74, 76–82, 88, 98, 106
  history of, 3, 6–8, 65–66, 72, 73
  kings and, 66, 81
  parliamentary control of, 69
  Roman, 7, 51, 69–70, 72–74, 76, 81–82, 106
  universal, 72, 76
Church of St. Nicolas du Chardonnet, 67
Church of Saint Sévérin, 67
Cicero, *De Officiis*, 43
citizens, 5, 9, 42, 63
Civil Wars of Religion, 2, 3, 5–7, 22, 62, 65, 70, 91, 97, 102, 105–6
Clément, Philippe, 2–3
clergy, 79–80, 88. *See also* popes; *specific clergy*
  ambition of, 76, 77–78
  corruption of, 75–76
Cletus, 63

Clovis, 74, 75
Coches Les, (Montaigne), 75
Collège de Clermont, 30
Collège de Presle, 3, 16, 27
Colloques d'Amour, 3
Commines, Philippe de, 44
Commynes, 7
concupisence, 56, 75
Condé, 94
confessional debate, 72
Conjuration of Amboise, 33
Constantinople, 8
Constitutions, 31
continuity, 6, 68, 69–70, 105–6. *See also* tradition
Copernicus, 56, 57
Correspondence (Pasquier), 9–10, 23–24, 30, 35, 66–67, 72, 95, 103, 105
Council of Trent, 66, 69, 70–71
Councils, 8
counselors, 35–36, 43, 49, 74–77. *See also* magistrates; statecraft
Cour de Cassation, 96–97
court, 49
Coutume de Paris, 103
Cujas, Jacques, 3, 28, 97
culture. *See* customs; tradition
customs, 33–64, 87, 103. *See also* tradition

Dahlinger, James H., *Etienne Pasquier on Ethics and History*, 10, 11
Darius, 39
De auferibilitate Papae ab Ecclesia (Gerson), 80
Decalogue, 8, 53
Défense et illustration, 5, 105
De Hoey, Jean, 4, 17, 25–26, 87
De l'Institution du prince (Budé), 37
Denis of Syracuse, 42–43, 46
De Officiis (Cicero), 43
Desan, Philippe, 26
Des Roches, Catherine, 4, 17–18, 25–28, 27
Des Roches, Madeleine, 4, 17, 25–28
Deuteronomy, 53
Diogenes, 40, 52
discontinuity, 6
Discours de la servitude volontaire (La Boétie), 50
disputatio, 33, 35, 36, 49–50, 54, 55, 56, 57, 59, 60–61, 64, 113n1
diversity, tolerance of, 49, 106
doctrinal apologetics, 7
doctrine, 7–9, 76
Dominicans, 88
Dorat, Jean, 5
Du Bellay, Joachim, 37, 113n14
  Défense et illustration, 5, 105
  Les Regrets, 76
Du Harlay, Achille, 94
Dupin, Claude, 10, 90, 94, 100, 104
  as "alter-Pasquier," 96–99
  Eloge d'Etienne Pasquier, 96–99
Du Tillet, Jean, 36, 70
Du Vair, Guillaume, 32

ecclesiology, 75
education, 43
Egypt, 46, 47
Elizabeth I, 28
Eloge d'Etienne Pasquier (Dupin), 96–99
Emilio, Paulo, 45
England, 30, 47, 82
Ephesians, 80
Ephestion, 39
Erasmus, Desiderius, 14, 25, 39, 53, 73
  In Praise of Folly, 40
Essais (Montaigne), 40, 75, 98
Estates of Blois, 1
Estates-General, 34
Estates of Orléans, 34
Estienne, Henri, 6, 94
ethics, 3, 5–7, 13, 53, 55–56, 60, 73, 87, 103, 105. *See also* values
"Etienne Pasquier" (Sainte-Beuve), 100
Etienne Pasquier on Ethics and History (Dahlinger), 10, 11
etymology, 6
Evangelicals, 81

exempla, 14–15, 37, 45, 79
Exodus, 53

faith, 6, 8, 57–58
Fauchet, Claude, 5, 26, 27, 28, 70
feudalism, 50
Feugère, Léon, 10, 97, 100
  Maitre, 10
  Oeuvres choisies d'Etienne Pasquier, 94–96, 100, 101
Fifth Republic, *National Assembly*, 104
Florilegia, 53
Formose, Pope, 78
fortune, 40, 41–42, 58, 61
Foulques, archbishop of Reims, 78
Fountainbleau, 34
Fragonard, Marie-Madeleine, 10, 84, 102
France. *See also* the Church, Gallican; French; Gallicanism
  culture of, 33–64, 65–66, 87, 100–101, 103, 105–6. *see also* continuity; tradition; values
  experience of, 100–101
  Gaulish origins of, 6
  history of, 44–45, 100–101, 103, 115n54
  laws of, 41–42, 44, 49–50, 57–58, 66, 68, 87, 99, 103
  national unity and, 66–67
  popes and, 65–66
  security of, 105–6
François I, 49, 91
François II, 6, 62, 83
freedom, 42
French, 37, 113–14n15
Froissart, 7

Gallicanism, 6–8, 30, 51, 65–66, 70–74, 76, 105–6. *See also* France
Garasse, François, 31, 87, 88, 95
  Recherches des Recherches et autres Oeuvres de M. Estienne Pasquier, por la défense de nos Roys, contre les ourages, calomnies et autres impertinences dudit auteur, Les, 9
gardens, metaphor of, 16–17
Gargantua (Rabelais), 62–63
Gaul, 66, 75
Gauls, 6, 48, 63, 77, 96
Geertz, Clifford, 15
Geneva, 67, 68
Germany, 30
Gerson, Jean, 79–81
  De auferibilitate Papae ab Ecclesia, 80
Ghibellines, 82
Giovio, Paolo, 7, 44
Giraud, Charles, 14, 31, 89–90, 93–97, 100, 104
Gnostics, 72
Gospels, 7, 53, 67, 106
Gournay, Marie De, 94
government. *See* statecraft
Grace, 8
Grands Jours, 4–5, 17, 25, 27, 87, 99
Greek, 37
Greeks, 63
Greenblatt, Stephen, 11, 13, 14, 15, 27, 29
Guelphes, 82
Guises, 62, 83

Hadrian, 37
Harlay, Achille du, 27
Henri II, 5, 22, 36, 59
Henri III, 2, 62, 91, 99
Henri IV, 31, 91, 92, 97, 105, 106
Henry V (England), 47
heresies, 66–67, 75
Hierosme, Saint, 75
Historia sui Temporis (Thou), 103
historiography, 7, 44–45, 103. *See also* France, history of
Holland, 30
Holy Decrees, 70
Horace, 43, 45
hubris, 63
Huguenots, 6, 34, 62, 73, 81–85, 106
Hugues Capet, 78, 83
humanism, 57
humors, 56
Huppert, George, 7, 10, 73, 106

individual, the, 33–64
In Praise of Folly (Erasmus), 40
Institution du prince (Budé), 43
institutional memory, 79–81
L'Interprétation des Institutes de Justinian (Pasquier), 10, 14, 89–94, 100
Irenaeus, St., 72, 76
irony, 61, 64
Italian literature, 23
Italian wars, 49
Italians, 51, 53–54, 55
Italy, influence of, 2, 50, 51, 53, 65–66, 68, 70–72, 101

Jardine, Lisa, 13, 14, 25
Jeanne d'Arc, 106
Jerusalem, 8
Jesuits, 4, 8–9, 29–31, 49, 67, 84–85, 88, 95, 97–98, 104, 106
judicial establishment, 58, 104. *See also* magistrates
Jules II, Pope, 81
Julius III, Pope, 30
July Monarchy, 94
jurist-poets, 25–28
justice, 34, 105

Keating, Clark, 102
kingship, 6, 31, 34–36, 38–50, 60–62, 90–91, 98, 106. *See also* statecraft
  authority of, 104
  Church and, 66, 81
  papacy and, 70–71, 75–77, 81–82
  responsibility of, 5
  rights and privileges of, 8
  Rome and, 76–77
  virtuous, 58

La Rochelle, 85
Latin, 37
Latinity, 101
La Vacquerie, 49
law, 2, 13, 33–64, 73, 103
  canon, 7
  changes to, 41–42, 57–58
  Christian tradition and, 65–85
  civil, 44
  continuity and, 68
  customary, 7, 99
  divine, 60
  ecclesiastical, 8, 77
  faith and, 57–58
  French, 7, 66, 87
  human, 60
  jurisprudence, 44
  Machiavellianism and, 41–42
  natural, 62
  permanent, 57–58
  regalian, 7
  religion and, 68, 79–81
  Roman, 7, 34, 44
  traditional, 41–42, 49–50, 99
  virtues and, 93
Law Faculty of Toulouse, 3
legitimate servitude, 105
Le Picard, Jean, 20
lettres, 37–38, 41, 92
Lettres (Pasquier), 88
Levasseur, maître du Collège du Cardinal Lemoine, 4
l'Hospital, Michel de, 6, 9, 33–35, 49, 58, 69, 84, 92, 104
l'Huillier, Pierre, 68
Ligue, 2, 3, 62, 92, 99, 106
liguers, 84
literature, 41, 45, 113–14n15. *See also specific authors and forms*
  ancient, 37–38
  Italian, 18–19, 23, 43
  medieval, 5
  Roman, 37–38
  women and, 21–24
Livy, 47
Loisel, Antoine, 3, 5, 7, 17, 27–29, 31, 94, 99, 104, 112n42, 113–14n15
  Pasquier, ou dialogue des avocats du parlement de Paris, 27, 93–94, 99
Lorraine, Charles de, 24–25, 29–30

Louis, Saint, 22
Louis Le Debonnaire, 77
Louis XI, 43, 44, 48–49
Louis XII, 44, 47, 81
Louis XIII, 91
Louis XVI, 89
Louis XVIII, 89
love, 75–76
Lumières, 88
Lutheranism, 8, 30, 81, 82, 84, 97, 105–6
Luxembourg, Jean de, 94
Lycurgus, 48, 57

Machiavellianism, 41–42, 46, 53
magistrates, 34, 43, 46, 94, 99
Magnien, Catherine, 3, 10, 102
"Main, la," 4
Main de Pasquier, La, 17, 25, 26, 27
Maitre (Feugère), 10
Malherbe, 32
Mangot, Claude, 32
Mangot, Louise, 32
Marcionites, 72
Maréchale de Retz, 21
Marie Stuart, Queen, 106
Marillac, Guillaume de, 21, 75
Marot, 79
marriage, 19–21, 47
Martel, Charles, 74, 76
medicine, 46, 49, 115n51
meditation, 40
memory, institutional, 79–81
mental hygiene, 18–19
Mesme, Henri de, 103, 104
metanoia, 55
metatextuality, 54
Mettayer, Jamet, 68
misogyny, 52, 115n50
modernity, 5, 7
Molé, Matthieu, 94
monarchy, 13, 35–36, 38–50, 67. *See also* kingship; princes; *specific kings*
  French, 34, 106
  monarchie de marque, 6, 8, 9, 11
  parliamentary, 8, 67
Monophile, Le, 3, 19
Montaigne, Michel de, 18, 26–27, 34, 50, 52, 55, 67, 75–76, 94, 100–101, 111n15
  Coches, Les, 75
  Essais, 40, 75, 98
More, Thomas, 19, 53

Naples, 44
National Assembly, 104
national unity, 66–67
necessity, 51
Nero, 37, 39, 43
Neville, H. Sir, 85
nineteenth century, Pasquier's reception during the, 87–88
nobility, 32, 39, 41, 114n23
Nuncio, 85

Occasional Verse (Pasquier), 9
Oeuvres (Pasquier), 31, 88
Oeuvres choisies d'Etienne Pasquier (Feugère), 10, 94–96, 100
Order of St. Michel, 27
Original Sin, doctrine of, 75
Ovid, 43

pacifism, 72
pallium, 77, 78–79
Pampluna, siege of, 2
Pantagruel (Rabelais), 62–63
Papacy, 2, 8, 66, 70–74, 78. *See also* Popes; *specific popes*
  authority of, 76–77, 81–82
  infallibility of, 75
  kings and, 70–71, 75–77, 81–82
Papal States, 77
Paracelsus, 56, 57, 105, 115–16n55
Parliament, 3–4, 6–10, 88–89, 95–99, 103–4, 106
  law and, 29–31, 34, 49, 58, 66, 69, 72, 75, 81, 84
  Pasquier and, 13, 16
  religion and, 66, 69, 72, 75, 81, 84
Parliamentarians, 9, 28, 33, 51, 58, 65, 92, 93, 100, 104, 106

parody, 61, 64
Pasquier, Antoine, 2–3
Pasquier, Etienne. *See also* Pasquier, Etienne, works of
  anti-Jesuit writings, 106
  appeals to reader, 67
  apprenticeship at Paris Bar, 4
  burial at Church of Saint Sévérin, 67
  character of, 18–19, 111n23
  commentaries on the Gospels, 106
  as defender of the state against invented enemies, 28–31
  De Hoey portrait of, 4, 17, 25–27
  diversions and, 17–18
  early goals and, 16–17
  early life of, 14, 16
  genealogy of, 2
  last sacraments of, 67
  later correspondence of, 16
  legacy of, 87–102, 104
  legal training of, 97
  lineage of, 14
  as magistrate, 99
  persona of, 84–85
  personal piety of, 67
  portraits of, 25–27, 87
  professional advancement of, 19–21
  reception in posterity, 9, 87–102
  salon life and, 17–18
  self-fashioning and, 13–15, 17–18, 84–85, 89
  sensibilities and, 16–17
  sons' careers and, 31–32
  style of, 58
Pasquier, Etienne, works of
  Catéchisme des jésuites, 10, 30, 85, 88, 106
  Correspondence, 9, 10, 23–24, 30, 35, 66–67, 72, 95, 103, 105
  L'Interprétation des Institutes de Justinian, 10, 14, 89–90, 100
  Lettres, 88
  de Pasquier, La Main, 17, 25, 26, 27
  Monophile, Le, 19
  Occasional verse, 9
  Oeuvres, 31, 88
  Oeuvres choisies d'Etienne Pasquier (Feugère), 10, 94–96, 100
  Poème de la Puce, 17, 25
  Pourparler d'Alexandre, 10–11, 59–64, 75, 97–98, 104–5
  Pourparler de la loy, 10–11, 50–59, 75, 97–98, 104–5
  Pourparler du prince, 10–11, 17–18, 35–49, 75, 97, 98, 104–5
  Recherches de la France, 10–11, 24–26, 30, 33, 36, 46–48, 54, 59, 60–61, 63, 65–74, 77–85, 88, 95–98, 100, 103, 105–6
  Ménippé, La Satire, 106
Pasquier, Etienne-Denis, 9–10, 89–95, 104
Pasquier, Françoise, 4
Pasquier, Guy, 4
Pasquier, Jean, 2
Pasquier, Nicolas, 4, 14, 31–32, 67, 87
  Lettres de Nicolas Pasquier, fils d'Estienne, Les . . . Avec la response aux Recherches des Recherches, 9
Pasquier, Pierre, 4, 14, 31–32
Pasquier, René, 4
Pasquier, Theodore, 4, 14, 31–32
Pasquier ou dialogue des avocats du parlement de Paris (Loisel), 27, 93–94, 99
Patristic Age, 7, 72
Paul, Saint, 76
Paul III, Pope, 30
Pauline Epistle, 80
Peloponnesian War, 38
penal justice, 105
Pepin, 74, 76, 77
Perron, Davy du, 106
Persia, 44
Persians, 63
persuasion, 72
Pertinax, 43
Peter, 71, 72, 76
Petrarch, 43
Petrarchan imitation, 18–19
Petrarchan sonnet, 19
Petrine office, 71, 72, 73

philosophers
  Greek, 51–52
  pre-Socratic, 57
philosophes, 102
philosophy, 55
Pibrac, Guy du Faur de, 34, 104
Pilate, 8
Pindar, 38
Pithou, François, 104
Pithou, Pierre, 3, 5, 7, 10, 14–17, 19, 23, 25, 27–28, 66, 70, 84, 88, 99, 104, 106
Plato, 38
  Republic, 36, 43, 46
Pléïade, 1, 5, 19, 32, 100, 105, 113n14
Poème de la Puce, 17, 25
poetry, 43
  Ancient Roman, 37–38
  French, 113–14n15
  Italian, 23
  medieval, 5
  women and, 21–24
Poitiers, 4–5, 17, 25, 31, 87, 99
political conduct, 103
politics, 60
politiques, 80, 84
popes, 9, 30, 38–39, 70, 73–74, 76–78, 106. *See also* Papacy; *specific popes*
  ambitions of, 72–73
  authority of, 70–73, 81–82
  duties of, 72–73
  France and, 65–66, 70–73
  infallibility of, 75
  kings and, 81–82
posterity, 63–64
post-Second Empire period, 104
Pourparler d'Alexandre (Pasquier), 3, 10–11, 33–35, 36, 41, 59–64, 75, 97–98, 104–5
Pourparler de la loy (Pasquier), 11, 33–35, 49, 50–59, 75, 97–98, 104–5
Pourparler du prince (Pasquier), 3, 4, 10–11, 17–18, 33–50, 75, 97–98, 105
pourparler genre, 33
Pragmatic Sanction of Bourges, 66
princes, 60–61, 63. *See also* kingship; monarchy
Protestantism, 30, 76, 81–85, 105–6. *See also specific sects*
Provençal sonnet, 23
proverbs, 6
Ptolemy, 43
public good, 31, 34, 35, 46
public servant, ideal, 13–32
"Puce de Madame Des Roches La," 4

Rabelais, François, 5, 40, 53, 59, 60–64, 79, 100, 105
  Gargantua, 62–63
  Pantagruel, 62–63
Ramus, Peter, 3, 27–28
Rapin, Nicholas, 17
Raymond, count of Toulouse, 37
readers, appeals to, 67
reading, 18–19
Recherches de la France (Pasquier), 24–26, 33, 36, 46–48, 50, 54, 59–61, 63, 95, 97–98, 100, 102–3, 105
  Book I, 5–6, 10–11, 42, 47, 68, 75, 96
  Book II, 8, 22, 60, 68, 73, 78
  Book III, 3, 6–9, 11, 30, 65–74, 77, 79–81, 84–85, 105–6
  Book IV, 17, 39, 42, 73
  Book VI, 106
  Book VII, 88
  Book VIII, 23, 73, 82–84, 106
  Gallicanism in, 70–74
  intentions of, 69
  tone of, 69
Reformation, 106
  Catholic, 76, 81
Reformers, 6, 76, 81, 82–84, 106
regency periods, 59–60
Les Regrets (Du Bellay), 76
religion, 3, 6, 9, 45, 103. *See also* the Church; *specific religious creeds*
  changes to, 105–6
  continuity and, 68, 69–70
  in France, 65–66
  law and, 68, 79–81
  religious ethics, 3
Republic (Plato), 36, 43, 46

Restoration, 89, 104
Richelieu (Armand Jean du Plessis), 91
Richeome, Louis, 85
rights, 7, 8, 70, 76
Robinot, Gilles, 50
robins, 4, 5, 103, 104, 106
Roche-Maillet, Gabriel Michel de la, 104
Roman de la rose, 38, 117n22
Rome, 6, 8, 43, 48, 51, 55
Ronsard, 5, 19, 76, 100, 105, 106
Roudaut, François, 10, 84, 102
royal conduct, 49
Royal Council, 34
Royal Ordinnances, 70

Sainte-Barbe, 2
Sainte-Beuve, Charles-Augustin, 10, 87, 88, 99–101
Causeries du lundi, 99–101
"Etienne Pasquier," 100
Saint-Séverin, Church of, 2
salon life, 27, 31
Satire Ménippé, La, 106
Sayhi-Périgot, Béatrice, 10, 38, 52, 54, 57, 61
Scévole de Sainte-Marthe, 104
Scotland, 47
Scriptures, 7, 53, 69, 72
Sebillet, Thomas, 23
security, 105–6
See of Rome, 8, 76–77
self-construction, 7
self-fashioning, 4, 7, 9, 10, 13–32, 22, 104
self-mastery, 40
self-reflection, 40
senses, 56–57
servitude, 50–51, 52, 105
sex, 54, 55
Seyssel, Claude de, 44, 47, 102
Sicily, 44
slaves, 50–53
Songe du vergier, Le, 71
sonnet form, 23, 52
Sophocles, 38
Sorbonne, 79–80
Spain, 2, 68
Sparta, 48
spirituality, 76
statecraft, 34, 35–36, 38–42, 44, 47, 49–50, 61–62, 105
St. Cyprien, 2
Stoics, 51–52
Sutto, Claude, 10, 85
Sylvester, 72

temporality, 76
Terror, the, 89
Tertullian, 72
Thales, 57
theology, 7
Thermidorian Reaction, 89
Thevet, André, 55
Thibaut IV, 37
Thickett, Dorothy, 10, 67, 85, 87, 88, 101–2, 106
Thou, Christophe de, 103, 104
Thou, Jacques-Auguste de, 7, 94, 103
Historia sui Temporis, 103
Thucidides, 38
Tiberius, 43
Toulouse, 16
Tournèbe, Adrien, 3
Tours, 84
tradition, 2, 6–7, 59, 64–65, 69
Trévoux Press, 9, 31, 87, 88
tricksters, 63
Troyes, 4, 17, 25, 27, 31
Turenne, Henri de la Tour d'Auvergne, vicomte de, 94
twentieth century, Pasquier's reception during the, 87–88, 99–101
Tyard, Pontus de, 1, 5, 104
Tyberius, 37

universities, 53, 106
University of Paris, 4, 29, 30, 31, 80, 84, 88, 97
Urfé, Honoré d', 32, 91

Valois Dynasty, 62, 83, 90
values, 34, 56, 59, 64–65, 69, 73, 87

vanity, 58
Vatican Council I, 75
Venetian Republic, 47–48
Verus, 43
vices, 38, 44, 48, 51, 75
Virgil, 38
virtues, 38, 51, 58, 63, 75, 93
Voltaire (François-Marie Arouet), 9, 88, 102
War of the Roses, 82
Western Christianity, 7–8
Western Schism, 79
women, 19–24, 115n50
world-upside-down, 52, 53, 58
writing, 18–19, 23

Xenocrates, 37

www.ingramcontent.com/pod-product-compliance
Ingram Content Group UK Ltd.
Pitfield, Milton Keynes, MK11 3LW, UK
UKHW021827100926
8556IPUK00003B/211

9 781433 120633